Praise for

THIS IS HOW WE PRAY

"*This Is How We Pray* is a beautifully written reminder of how prayer is first and foremost about friendship with God. Dressler doesn't try to prescribe certain prayers, or dive deep into the theology of prayer, instead he shares how prayer can become a vital and important part of our lives, every single day. Go read this book!"

—Mark Batterson, *New York Times* bestselling
author of *The Circle Maker*, lead pastor
of National Community Church

"Adam goes under the spiritual hood straight to the engine and examines our connection to the true source of strength. The human heart's engagement with God is the most resisted because it has the most potential. This book on prayer aims at nothing less than paradise regained."

—Jared Anderson, singer, songwriter, worship leader

"Adam takes a mysterious and essential subject of the Christian faith and makes it easy to apply in an honest and practical way. This is a must read for anyone who wants to deepen and strengthen their prayer life."

—Matt McCoy, founder of LoopCommunity.com

"Prayer is this strange thing that few of us feel we know how to do, yet we all end up doing it anyway. We treat it like algebra, but it's more like breathing. Adam Dressler knows this truth in his bones, and he opens that truth into a million other truths in this wise but easygoing collection of reflections. Dressler won't teach you to pray, exactly, but he will help you see how you're already praying—and how you're actually made for it, and have been all along."

—Patton Dodd, coauthor of *The Prayer Wheel:*
A Daily Guide to Renewing Your Faith
with a Rediscovered Spiritual Practice

"Like an experienced trail guide, Dressler meets us where we are and leads us on the journey of prayer with a disarming style and piercing wisdom. He clears through the brush of formulas and rules, keeps us on well-worn paths of intimacy with God, and lifts our eyes to the breathtaking beauty of a deep life with God."

—Glenn Packiam, author of *Discover the Mystery of Faith*
and the forthcoming *Blessed Broken Given*

This Is
How We Pray

This Is How We Pray

Discovering a Life of Intimate Friendship with God

ADAM DRESSLER

New York   Nashville

FaithWords
Hachette Book Group
1290 Avenue of the Americas, New York, NY 10104
faithwords.com
twitter.com/faithwords

Originally published in hardcover and ebook by FaithWords in March 2019
First trade paperback edition: March 2020

FaithWords is a division of Hachette Book Group, Inc. The FaithWords name and logo are trademarks of Hachette Book Group, Inc.

The publisher is not responsible for websites (or their content) that are not owned by the publisher.

The Hachette Speakers Bureau provides a wide range of authors for speaking events. To find out more, go to www.hachettespeakersbureau.com or call (866) 376-6591.

Library of Congress Cataloging-in-Publication Data

Names: Dressler, Adam, author.
Title: This is how we pray : discovering a life of intimate friendship with God / Adam Dressler.
Description: first [edition]. | New York : Faith Words, 2019. | Includes bibliographical references.
Identifiers: LCCN 2018044404| ISBN 9781546035046 (hardcover) |
    ISBN 9781546035039 (ebook)
Subjects: LCSH: Prayer—Christianity. | Spirituality—Christianity. | Spiritual life—Christianity.
Classification: LCC BV210.3 .D74 2019 | DDC 248.3/2—dc23
LC record available at https://lccn.loc.gov/2018044404

ISBNs: 978-1-5460-3505-3 (trade paperback), 978-1-5460-3503-9 (ebook)

Printed in the United States of America

LSC-C

10 9 8 7 6 5 4 3 2 1

For everyone who tries to pray,
or at least wants to.

CONTENTS

The wish to pray is a prayer in itself.
                                    —*Georges Bernanos*[1]

I believe that everyone is interested in prayer, even if only marginally. Prayer is one of those things that continues to remain universal, throughout different times and places. We know that we aren't alone. Whether it's through religion or astronomy or a hike in the woods or a boat on the open water, we want to reach out to whatever else is out there in the universe, hoping to make contact with something that affirms what we already know—that there are parts of our insides that simply cannot accept that life is merely physical. So we stretch out our hearts, in whatever ways we know how, to try to connect with whatever exists outside of our physical lives.

Is this not the basis of every prayer ever prayed?

There are numerous books on prayer that men and women far more advanced in its art and mystery than I am have already written. So why *another* one?

Books about prayer tend to fall into a few categories. Some

of these books are written from a place of theology, meaning that their authors set out to explore the many different beliefs that inform why we should pray, and what we should think about prayer. Other books are written from a place of practice—their authors focus more on the devotional aspect of prayer, exploring the specific techniques we can strive to master in order to experience a deeper, more fulfilling life of prayer.

I want to get this out there from the beginning: this book will probably fail at both of these. I am neither an expert theologian, equipped with the knowledge and intellect to wrestle prayer into a submission of the mind, nor a particularly pious man, armed with a quiver of rapturous prayer experiences that will move your heart.

The truth is, I am a fairly average person. I grew up in a typical Midwestern home. My mother raised us kids in our small-town Presbyterian church, faithfully taking us to worship services on most Sunday mornings, modeling for us the importance of things like singing hymns, giving some of your money to God, and spending an extra half-hour in the church lobby after everyone else has already left so you can talk with the elderly widow who is lonely and just wants someone to listen to her share about her flowers and her sons and how much she misses her husband.

My father is a generous man who worked hard and made sure that we never wanted for anything and, in his own way, modeled for us a different kind of faith. It wasn't until much later in his life that he began a relationship with God, showing us that it's never too late to start something new and that God answers our prayers. But sometimes he takes his time.

I say all of this to let you in a bit on who is actually writing these words—which is important. I want you to know that I didn't grow up the son of a preacher. I didn't spend my vacations in a monastery. I've never led a crusade and I am surprisingly ineffective in most of the evangelistic attempts I make. I have shockingly little of the Bible memorized. As you will see in this book, I often prefer sleeping in over getting up early to pray, and in many ways, I am still very much a beginner in the mystery of prayer.

But in some sense, *aren't we all?*

If God is who he says he is, then we should never be surprised by our own sense of inadequacy when we are around him. This is the God who crafted the universe. This is the God who rules over it all. Nothing in our human lives can even remotely compare to his power, his responsibility, his grandeur.

What is amazing about this God is that he stoops to our level in something called "prayer." He voluntarily sets aside his great other-ness and opens the door for us to come in. In short, he makes room for us.

If you're like me, prayer is something you both long to experience in a deeper way and, at the same time, ironically avoid because most of the time it just seems *so hard*. Because it's in prayer that we encounter not only this grand, all-powerful God, but also our frail, broken selves. Prayer often keeps with it a companion of discouragement. Prayer *is* hard.

So I'm writing to those of us (yes, I'm including myself here) who have struggled to find a life of prayer that satisfies us, difficulties and all. My hope is a simple one. I want to talk about what prayer feels like—its wide scope of pressure points that, although discomforting, are actually designed to bring us closer to the God we want to know, the God we want to love.

This is not a technical book, per se. Meaning that I'm not writing about how to simply pray *better*. Of course, I hope this book leads you to pray in more meaningful ways. Me, too. But any ground we can gain in our prayer lives will be a result of first exploring why prayer is often so discouraging, and how God uses these feelings of discouragement to shape us. Then, we end up finding that these very feelings of discouragement have another, hidden purpose. They shape us into creatures of hope. As we experience the difficult realities of prayer, and as we continue to pray (or try to pray) in the midst of those difficult realities, we also experience another, greater reality at the same time: God is there. And not only is he there. He is there with us as a friend.

It should probably also be said from the beginning that I tend to think any progress we make toward building something of value will usually follow after an intentional, maybe even painful, time of tearing some things down—of discovering how things really are, even if it's a painful discovery. Or another way to say this is that before we build our dream home, we have to first tear down the old eyesore of a shed on the land, to make room.

This, then, is what this book is about. *Making room.* God making room for us. Us making room for God. And hopefully, through this process, we become more like the kinds of people that he designed us to become—people who know firsthand what it means to not only experience but *enjoy* an intimate relationship with the divine creator of our souls.

1 FRIENDSHIP

AT SOME POINT while I was in college, I either read or heard this famous line: "If you want to humble a man, ask him about his prayer life." I later learned that it (most likely) came from Scottish minister Alexander Whyte. I do not know anything about Alexander Whyte, and I am not even Scottish. But I think he summarizes what most of us *feel* when we think about prayer. It is hard. It is humbling.

Prayer is an arena in which we must come to terms with who we really are. This is just one of the reasons why prayer is often so difficult for most of us mere mortals, and perhaps the most important one. In prayer, we hope to have our highest ideals and ambitions of spiritual growth and connection realized. Regardless of our age or spiritual maturity, we are all like six-year-olds. We want to somehow experience *wonder*. Specifically, we want to experience wonder *with God*. We want to put on our shoes, zip up our jackets, and hike to the highest ridge we can find. We then want to sit down on a bench, let out a slow sigh, and stare off into a big horizon.

We want to feel noble, but at the same time, we want to

feel small. In our smallness, we want to feel like we are in the presence—the hands—of something bigger than ourselves. We want to know there is someone who will call us up into his lap and wrap us up in his arms and tell us that he loves us and cares for us and is making everything okay. In short, we want to be *loved*.

But this is not the complete picture of who we are. Yes—we have the innocence of a six-year-old. But we also have the weakness of a wounded soldier. The vengeance of a betrayed captain. The selfishness of an angry toddler. The despair of an imprisoned criminal. The distraction of a bee surrounded by hundreds of spring flowers. The surliness of a forgotten hospital patient.

And this is the hard part of prayer. We know that we are told to pray—and that we *should* pray. But which one of us is doing the praying here? Is it the innocent version of ourselves, asking for the Kingdom? Or is it the bored version of ourselves asking for God to show off? Or is it the angry version of ourselves asking for a bear to come and eat our enemies? Or is it the hurting version of ourselves asking for the Great Surgeon to stop the cutting and finally end his operation?

Yes.

To all of these, yes.

Søren Kierkegaard once said that a purity of heart is to will one thing. This is one of those statements that grows larger the more you think about it. It at least means that our hearts are fractured things that scatter their thoughts and feelings in a thousand different directions, some good and some bad, and this fracturing process leaves us *feeling* fractured. Because of our fractured condition, we suffer from a near-constant crisis in identity. Or better said, *identities*. We don't always know who we are. As Brennan Manning has said:

> When I get honest, I admit I am a bundle of paradoxes. I believe and I doubt, I hope and get discouraged, I love and I hate, I feel bad about feeling good, I feel guilty about not feeling guilty. I am trusting and suspicious. I am honest and I still play games. Aristotle said I am a rational animal; I say I am an angel with an incredible capacity for beer.[1]

The great poet Walt Whitman says the same thing in his famous poem "Song of Myself":

> *Do I contradict myself?*
> *Very well then I contradict myself;*
> *(I am large, I contain multitudes)*[2]

If you have ever made any serious attempt at prayer, you know how true all of this is. Prayer is hard because it requires us to come to terms with our own fractured hearts. Our own paradoxes. Our own contradictions. We want to be "spiritual," but we also want to sleep in. We want to be selfless, but we also want things to go our way. We want to love others, but we also want our sister to stop drinking and calling to tell us how unfair her life is seven times a day. We want to grow in our patience, but we also want that parking space next to the door because it's raining and we wore our good shoes today and our toddler is having a breakdown in the back because he wants us to let him take his toy car into the store and we won't let him, and now he's screaming bloody murder at us, and people are starting to stare and we just need one thing to go right today because it's been a really, really tough week.

So prayer is challenging. Because prayer requires something in us to settle down and admit who we are. Which can be exhausting at best, crushing at worst. Something that is meant to give us life and joy and satisfaction and fulfillment too often, quite honestly, exposes our weakness and takes too much from us. Who needs another thing to fail at? Who needs another reminder of how weak we are? Who needs another source of shame in our lives?

And yet.

We can't give it up. Every day millions of people across the world pause whatever they are doing and, as best as they can, lift up their fractured, weakened, shame-filled hearts to God. They ask him for the gift of feeling small. They ask to be held by his hands. They ask to be heard by his holy audience.

Why is that? Why can't we just wash our hands and be done with all of this prayer business? Why do dying men utter words to a God they might not even know? Why do artists and athletes give quick credit to God when they achieve a marker of success? Why do addicts with fresh needle tracks in their arms keep asking this same God to help them get clean, even though they have asked for that help hundreds of times before without any clear progress being made?

There are lots of possible answers to these questions. But perhaps the one that matters most is the one that I, like the dying man and the young mom and the athlete and the addict, experience in the deepest, truest places of my heart: *I want to know that I am not alone.* I want to know that my life and all of its pains and struggles, all of its victories and celebrations, are not solitary endeavors. There is something in me that longs to know—desperately, even frantically at times—that my story is a shared one. That someone else sees me, hears me, knows me, and walks with me. I want an assurance that I am not left to my own resources as I try to figure out what I'm facing, what I'm feeling, and what I'm fearing.

I want a *friend*.

Ultimately, this is what I'm after in prayer. I think that's what most people are after, too. We all want someone to see us, love us, accept us, and desire to be with us. Just as we are. Just as we *really* are.

Peter Kreeft gives me a lot of hope in my search for a better prayer life when he says very simply that prayer is friendship with God.[3] Even as I write these five words, something inside me says, *Yes. That's exactly what I want it to be.* I don't want prayer to be a system that I can manipulate or, even worse, fail at. I don't want prayer to be a duty or an obligation. I don't want prayer to be a one-sided conversation. I want it to be a true friendship between myself and God. That's it. I want prayer to be a living, breathing part of my life that travels with me throughout my days.

When I was seventeen, I flew from my childhood home in Ohio to Tulsa, Oklahoma, for a college visit. As soon as my plane descended for landing, I looked out the window and saw the largely barren Midwestern landscape below me and said a simple "Nope." When I arrived on campus, my intention to reject Tulsa and the college I was visiting only grew. There was no way I was going to spend "the best four years of my life" here.

But then I met my roommate for the week, Robbyn. The admissions office had assigned me to his room for my stay. We introduced ourselves, made light small talk, shared a bit of our stories—"You're from Ohio? I'm from Mississippi." "Cool."—and then we went to grab dinner. Over the next two days we became friends. So much so that before I left, we decided to room together the following year, if I decided to enroll.

I ended up enrolling. And Robbyn and I lived together for a year, then lived next door to each other two years later. He is a year older than I am, so he graduated a year before me. Anxious to see the world, he spent several years overseas, working in Europe and the Middle East. Life went on, we both married, both went to graduate school, and now we both find ourselves as fathers raising young children and trying to cope with the fact that we are no longer young anymore.

We have stayed close—at times closer than others—throughout each of these seasons of our lives. We have known each other for almost twenty years. He has seen me at my worst. I have seen him at his worst. As one of my counselors once said, "You know you are really enjoying a true friendship when you have enough dirt [except he didn't say "dirt"] on someone to completely ruin their lives, if you ever wanted to. And they could do the same to you."

This is what I experience with a friend like Robbyn.

A true friendship.

And this is what I want with God. Not the ruining each other's lives part. But the long, steady presence in my life that is not dependent on my being perfect, or even good enough to be considered trustworthy. Or even just worthy. I want to experience a long, steady walk with a God who knows me—all of me—and yet still sticks around.

This is why I pray.

I'm guessing this is why you pray, too. I'm guessing this is why you are reading this book. You want to become God's friend. In all of your fractured identities and disordered loves and selfish desires and spiritual wanderings, the one thing that you want—or maybe even just *want* to want—is a friendship with God.

If we take Jesus on his own terms, we have to take seriously his startling assertion that he, in fact, calls us his *friends*.

Let that sink in for a minute.

The God of the universe calls you *friend*.

In many ways, prayer is our heart's journey to find out what this means.

2 REACHING

PHILIP YANCEY WROTE a book called *Reaching for the Invisible God*, which accurately describes how most people feel when they try to pray. First, there is the reaching part. We muster up some courage and dare to connect with a God we aren't entirely sure we believe in, let alone trust. But we have heard about him. We have heard that he wants to hear from us. So we stretch out our souls through our words, whether spoken audibly or silently, and we ask this cosmic stranger to make himself known to us. We are aware of our own smallness. We are vaguely aware of this stranger's bigness. And like a small child longing for the comfort of his parent's hand, we unclasp our fingers, open up our palms, and reach.

We reach when it's the end of the month and we open the day's mail and find the unexpected bill—*God, how am I going to pay this?* We reach when we are in our beds at night next to a sleeping spouse and all we feel is angry and alone—*God, how can I keep going like this?* We reach when we're running late for a meeting and the Ford Focus in front of us is going ten miles under the speed limit and there's a truck next to us on the right and double yellow lines next to us on the left and then we hit the red light—*God, fix this now!*

Reaching out for help is one of the most common ways that we pray. We find ourselves living in a world that is frustrating at best, unbearable at worst, and we look for some way to find relief. Crying out for God to help us is the most native of all prayers, like a newborn baby crying out for her mother to hold her.

We also reach out when we see our prayers answered, like when we have time away at a beach—*Thank you God for giving us a good vacation.* We reach out when we experience something beautiful—*God, this sunset is almost too much to take in.* We reach out when we find ourselves in the middle of something good that we didn't deserve—*God, thank you for this friendship.*

Gratitude is another basic emotion that causes us to reach out to God. When we experience good things in our lives, most of us will, at one time or another, ask this very innocent and honest question: *Who gave these things to me?* Even if we are unsure about the answer, we still see the good things in our lives as coming from somewhere outside ourselves. And we are grateful.

The last major way that we reach out to God is different than all of these, because it is motivated by guilt. In his classic address *Mere Christianity*, C. S. Lewis opens his exploration into faith by giving his readers an example of two people arguing.[1] Except he says "quarrelling" because he is British, and like most British people, he naturally makes his point in the most refined way possible. Lewis notes that in every quarrel (read: argument), the two sides involved make an appeal to right and wrong as a means of justifying their behaviors. While their arguments may contain appeals to personal preferences— "Why did you fold the towels like *that?*"—the real reason why someone argues at all is because he has it in his mind that the other person has *wronged him in some way*.

Lewis's point is that we can't help ourselves. Every single human being has imprinted on his or her heart the notion of right and wrong. Some people call this "morality." Others call it "conscience." Others call it the "fear of God." Regardless of whatever we call it, we can't escape it. Across all cultures, across all generations, the common experience of humanity is that there are things we *should* do and things we *shouldn't* do. Everyone has the built-in capacity to feel an *ought*—as in, *I ought to be less selfish, I ought to honor my marriage vows, I ought to say "Hello" and smile at my elderly neighbor even though she put up a wind chime right outside my bedroom window and I'm a light sleeper and now I wake up in the middle of the night to the sound of a metal disc clanging against seventeen other, louder metal cylinders.* We know that we should do these kinds of things. And more.

The other point that Lewis makes is that, in addition to this sense of right and wrong that everyone feels (and lives by), we also have another sense working within us at the same time. And it is the reason why so many of us wrestle with deep feelings of fear, anxiety, restlessness, loneliness, sadness, and unhappiness. Here it is: *we cannot live the lives we know we ought to live.* We are selfish. We want to ignore our marriage vows. Instead of saying "Hello" and smiling to our elderly neighbor, we want to stare her down with shame and then we want to sneak out to the side of our house one night and throw that wind chime far, far away.

Simply put, we cannot be good enough. Good enough for others. Good enough for ourselves. Good enough for God. And we know that. Very acutely. In many ways, some subtle and some not, we try to cover this knowledge up and live as if there weren't a right and a wrong, live as if we don't fail as much as we do. But that is a doomed project from the beginning, because we only hurt ourselves when we fail to deal with life without a firm commitment to seeing things as they really are. Lewis writes as much when he says:

> These, then, are the two points I wanted to make. First, that human beings, all over the earth, have this curious idea that they ought to behave in a certain way, and cannot really get rid of it. Secondly, that they do not in fact behave in that way. They know the Law of Nature; they break it. These two facts are the foundation of all clear thinking about ourselves and the universe we live in.[2]

So this is another reason why we reach out to God. We feel guilty. We don't behave the way we should, and we know it. We pray to God as a means of making atonement for our shortcomings. We ask God to forgive us for being so selfish. We ask him to pardon us for wanting to ignore our marriage vows and to give us strength to carry on. We ask him to bless our elderly neighbor with the wind chime and not to judge us too harshly for just wanting to get some good sleep.

In a very real sense, this is what it means to pray: to reach for God.

And then there's the invisible part.

We take our desires for things to be different, our heartfelt expressions of gratitude, our deep need for forgiveness, and we package them up into something called "prayer" and send them off to ... where?

Unlike a conversation with a friend, prayer is, by nature, an exercise in the absurd. Meaning, when we share a table and a cup of coffee with a flesh-and-blood friend, we might not be confident that we are being understood, we might not be confident that we are even being heard, and we might still feel lonely in their presence. But even in the most misunderstood, most unempathetic, loneliest conversations we have with another person, what we can be confident of is that we both experience the same reality. We both sit in chairs. We both drink coffee. We both hear each other's voices. We both are present in the same place, together.

But prayer challenges all of this for us. We pour out our hearts, sometimes even with coffee in hand, but how can we be sure that we are speaking to someone real? How can we be sure that the God we are praying to is even in the room? How can we be sure that he even exists at all?

And that's what I mean by absurd. If you were to have no prior knowledge of prayer or religion or anything spiritual at all—if you were what philosophers called a "materialist," meaning that you only believed in a physical, observable universe—and you watched someone pray out loud in front of you, would

you not be a little unsettled? Would you not say that the act of praying looked and sounded absurd? Crazy, even?

Who are you talking to?

Why do you think you are being heard right now?

There's no one else in this room but me and you.

There's no one in this room who can bring world peace, who can heal your brother of cancer, who can ensure that your choice of a career will lead you to fulfillment and happiness.

Who are you thanking right now? The ceiling tiles?

Why are you apologizing?

Your husband isn't even here. Your neighbor isn't here. Your father isn't here. The woman with the four kids in the checkout line at the grocery who you say you silently judged isn't here.

Countless times in my life, I have experienced the haunting absurdity of prayer like this. Sometimes it is all I can do to believe that I am not alone in the room, in the car, in the shower, on the trail in the woods. Because it feels like I am praying to an invisible God, if he is a God at all. I don't see him. I don't hear him. I don't even sense his presence. I just sit there, spilling—sometimes hemorrhaging—out my heart to an empty room. Hoping that my greatest fear isn't, in fact, true: that I am *alone.*

Sometimes I try to trick my heart into believing something different than my fears. I play the Billy Graham tape through my head—the one where he boldly asserts that he has never seen the wind, but he has seen the effects of the wind, so he knows the wind exists. I try to self-warm my heart with thoughts about how God was "clearly there" for me. I think about the car wreck when I was sixteen. And then the one when I was twenty. I think about the time I was flying to Chicago from Denver and the plane felt like it was falling from the sky like a dead bird. I think about my emergency appendectomy. I think about my daughter and the almost two years of infertility before that.

God, that was you.

You were there.

Even though I couldn't see you.

You were there.

Sometimes this kind of exercise works. And I somehow have enough faith to believe that my prayers are actually heard. That they do make it past the ceiling tiles.

But other times, no matter how hard I try, I can't fake it. I can't make my heart believe something that it doesn't. I can't be strong enough to overcome my weaknesses of doubt, unbelief, and loneliness.

God, why don't you show yourself?

Why don't you speak?

Why do you stay silent?

Why do you remain invisible?

No one knows the answers to these questions. Anyone who says they do is lying. And that's actually a good thing that no one knows the answers, because if there is a God, he needs to be so infinitely smarter and so comprehensively better and so far above me that I can't figure him out. Imagine what it was like to live on this earth before we had the famous earth-rise picture taken from the moon. Or imagine if you lived on this earth before you knew it was round. If someone asked you how big the world was, you would literally have no way to give an even semi-intelligent answer. It would be impossible to speak accurately about the world and its place within the universe because your size and perspective relative to it would be so cosmically outmatched. How does a human being comprehend the galaxies? Or to put it another way, how does a microbe on the skin of an elephant comprehend the Sahara desert?

I don't have an answer for the invisible aspects of God's existence. I don't know why he doesn't show himself more clearly to us. Like the prophet Isaiah, I can only say, "You are a God who hides himself" (Isaiah 45:15).

This is just one of the realities that makes prayer so difficult. When we pray, we encounter this troubling paradox: we try to pray so that we can grow in our faith and belief in God. But the very act of praying requires faith and belief in God— faith and belief that we often don't have.

The only way forward I can see in this paradox is that we keep on reaching. Even if God seems invisible. Even if he seems distant. Even if he seems deaf. Even if he seems dumb. We keep reaching not because we believe. We keep reaching because we *don't* believe.

If prayer shows us anything, it shows us that we lack the power to believe in God the way that we feel like we should. Prayer reveals to us our poverty of spiritual things. But thank God that he loves the poor.

Blessed are the poor in spirit, for theirs is the kingdom of heaven. (Matthew 5:3)

3 DISTRACTIONS

ONE NIGHT AFTER getting our three kids in bed, I headed to bed myself.[1] I had every intention of getting some good rest so that I could wake up early the next morning to try and be spiritual. I planned to wake up around six, make some coffee, grab my Bible and a small journal I keep, sit in a quiet house, and meet with God.

First, our son was up. He is only five, but he has what nice people call "a voice that carries." He came out of his room, booming the bold declaration that he couldn't sleep and that he wasn't tired and by the way he couldn't find his ChapStick and it was probably gone forever and how could he possibly go to sleep without it?

Then our seven-year-old daughter was up. She came out of her room troubled by the fact that her comforter was covering her legs and making her too hot to sleep. It never occurred to her to use the two things she called "legs" that are attached to her to kick said comforter off. Instead, she felt it necessary to inform her parents that she needed us to do it. Never mind the fact that she used said legs to kick off the comforter in order to get out of bed to come let us know that the comforter was covering her and it was making her too hot.

And then our youngest daughter was up. She had just turned two, which meant she was getting some new teeth, which also meant that she was generally uncomfortable, especially at night. She cried from her crib. Hard. My wife tried to console her a bit in her room, but our daughter was having none of that. She knew my wife and I were still up, and if we were both allowed to enjoy the rest of the house, why shouldn't she be allowed the same freedom? So my wife brought her out to the kitchen to get her some water and then tried to calm her down a bit. Our daughter was still upset, and somehow she ended up in our bed, next to me, watching *Ramona and Beezus* on my phone.

The phone detail is important. My phone has a big screen for a phone, but a small screen for a two-year-old watching a movie. So picture me holding my phone at my daughter's eye level while she is half-sitting up, half-lying down in our bed, just so she can see. Anytime I would nod off and fall back asleep, my hand would inevitably sink down and drop the phone. Our daughter didn't care for that so much and would proceed to wake me up with a loud cry or a smack to the face or a gouge to the eye. This went on for an hour and a half—the full length of the movie.

Eventually she fell asleep, but it was late. And the night was not a peaceful one, as she woke up several times in pain, crying. When she wasn't crying, she was sleeping with her head next to her mom's. Which meant that her feet were in my ribs. Or in my neck.

My wife and I both slept through our alarms. I finally woke up when my son sauntered into our room at 6:30, telling—not asking—me to get up and get him some milk. And also to turn on the TV so he could watch a show.

Needless to say, nothing spiritual happened that morning. Even if I wanted to do something spiritual, where would I fit it in? Part of being a parent means that you make breakfast, you brush teeth, you pick out clothes, and you take kids to school. Whatever plans you have for a morning, even if they include being spiritual, quickly and most certainly unravel.

By the time I got into my office, I was already tired. I looked at my Bible and my small journal as I reached for my laptop. Everything within me wanted to start my work for the day. I already felt anxious and behind. But there was this nagging feeling of guilt-infused devotion when I opened up my computer.

Come to me, all who labor and are heavy laden, and I will give you rest. (Matthew 11:28)

I should pray.
But I am so tired.
And I have so much to do.
In my line of work as a pastor, sometimes I am around other pastors who make this sad and clichéd joke: "Pastoring would be great if it weren't for all of the people." Pastors usually

say this little quip to ease the tension of our daily realities. Working with people is sometimes demanding and long and messy and often unappreciated. Most pastors want to serve in this type of vocation because they love God and love to study and think and maybe even love to preach. The problem is that the God we love so much told us that we can't love him very well if we aren't willing to love his people. Deeply. Sacrificially. And if we are halfway competent at the preaching part of our jobs, people will keep showing up to hear us. Which means that we will, sooner or later, have to accept and even cherish the unavoidable fact that to be a pastor inherently means that we are involved with people.

It is the same with our prayer life. Most of us who want to make prayer a priority in our lives do so because we love God. Or at least we want to love God. But we don't come to this place of loving God in a vacuum. Surrounding our love for God is all the other stuff of life. We have kids to care for. We have marriages to work on. We have lawns to mow and garages to clean and groceries to buy and text messages to return and *Ramona and Beezus* to watch on our phones in the middle of the night as we try to stay awake so our two-year-old remains relatively calm.

Prayer and, more broadly, loving God, would be so much easier if we didn't have to deal with everything else. The challenge of living a spiritual life is that so much of our lives is seemingly unspiritual. The unspiritual parts cover our spiritual desires with an almost oppressive weight at times. We catch glimpses of our spiritual desires every once in a while. But for the most part, we relegate them to the future, or a vision for a better version of our lives, and instead focus our energies on just getting everything else *done*.

How do we pray in the midst of our daily lives?

How are we supposed to pray when we can barely keep our eyes open?

How are we supposed to sit and be still when we have so much to do?

One of the ways I try to answer these questions is through fantasy. When we hear the word *fantasy*, we usually think of something related to romance, but I'm not talking about that kind of fantasy. I'm talking about an idyllic escape where I am free to do whatever I want.

My prayer fantasy goes something like this: I'm in the most comfortable bed I've ever slept in and the temperature of the room is cool, but not cold. I'm sleeping on sheets made from Egyptian cotton. Why that makes them good, I don't know, but that's what I always hear in commercials and on hotel websites. I'm cozy under a down comforter and my pillow is the perfect size and shape—no lumps.

There is a large, clear window facing east, so the sun can beam in with no interruptions. As the first few rays of the rising sun start their spread over the sleepy world, I wake up. Without an alarm. I just slowly open my eyes and...I'm awake. I peel off the comforter, but I'm not cold because someone has put warmed flannel slippers at the foot of my bed, along with a warm flannel robe.

No one else is awake yet. And I am confident that they will

stay asleep, so I don't even have to tiptoe down the hallway to the kitchen, where I grind my fresh coffee beans, bring some water to a near-boil, and make some coffee.

By now the sun has crept high enough to light up the wispy clouds left over from the night before. I can still see the moon. Coffee in hand, I grab my Bible and small journal and head out to a deck that faces east. I'm surrounded by pine trees and a cool morning chill. Off in the distance I see a snow-covered mountain. I hear birds. There is a small fire lit in a fire pit by my feet that keeps me warm and gives me something to stare at besides the sun and the mountains and the trees and the steam rising from my coffee.

I turn to a Psalm or one of the Gospels and start to read. After reading a few lines, I pause and pray. *God, what are you trying to show me about yourself right now? What are you trying to say to me? How do I need to see you? How do I need to see myself?* I read a few more lines, and then pause and pray again.

In between reading like this and taking sips of my coffee, I jot down a few thoughts or prayers in my journal. Nothing too heavy or long. Just a few small ideas I want to remember.

After an hour or so of just sitting and praying like this, my wife and children wake up. And I go on about my day with a full heart, a full spirit. Steady. Centered. Assured of God's love and presence in my life.

Or I can go the complete opposite way, too. When I was in college, I took a class on the monastic movements of the Middle Ages. In this class, I read about how some men and women of God left all the comforts of the world so that they could settle (or attempt to settle) the deepest questions and longings of their hearts. They lived simple and intentional lives in an effort to limit the number of distractions they faced.

So sometimes my prayer fantasy looks like this: me sitting in a room, alone, with only a candle as my companion. I'm wearing some type of robe. I've got a Bible and maybe a small journal, and maybe there's a desk or a chair or a bed of some sort. But the room is sparse and small and completely free of distractions. The kind of room that seems to instill holiness into its occupants. I don't have anything else. It's just me. In a room. With God.

I call these two ideas fantasies because that's exactly what they are. Both of these pictures are so far from my daily reality. When I pray in the mornings, it usually looks something like this: I wake up late—or at least, later than I wanted—and I am tired. Dead tired. I try to be as helpful as I can with getting the kids ready for the day and then I take a quick shower. Under the falling water, I try to direct my tired heart toward God. I ask him for help. I try to thank him for another day. I remember the day before and I tell him I'm sorry for being such a self-centered human being. Then, in the midst of these short, halfhearted prayers, I usually hear my son banging on the bathroom door, asking me what I'm doing—*I'm taking a shower and trying to connect WITH THE GOD OF THE UNIVERSE!*—and if I can come help him with something. I finish up getting ready, and head off to work.

Regardless of what my prayer fantasy specifically looks like, the common idea behind it is that I am away from all the things that happen around me that seem to make a meaningful prayer life so hard.

Let me be clear: I love my family. Most days. I love my job. Most days. I don't mind going to the grocery or getting the oil changed in our van or watching *Ramona and Beezus* for the thirty-seventh time. But these things, in their own way, sometimes seem to stand as obstructions to what I want in my life: intimacy with God. Intimacy that comes only from a life of prayer that reaches into my flesh and blood.

The temptation we face is to think that by eliminating these outward distractions we would somehow be a different kind of person than what we currently are. We think that we would be godlier, more focused on spiritual things, less self-centered.

Throughout my life, I have seen that this idea simply is not true. While it is tempting to think that the external realities of our lives are the real reasons why we suffer from such spiritual weaknesses, we are deceiving ourselves. That line of thinking is a type of spiritual shell game where we are being tricked before the game even begins. We think that life is somehow stacked against us being spiritual. And if we could somehow clear out some of the things we have in our lives that keep us from being spiritual, we would finally make real progress in our relationship with God.

Instead of blaming the external circumstances of our lives for our spiritual poverty, we should ask this question instead:

Who gave us this life we have anyway?

And then:

Who put these kids in my house that wake up early and demand their milk and a show?

Who gave me this job and all these problems that need to be solved?

Who created this body that gets tired and cranky and aches?
God did.

God gave you every boundary and constraint and reality in your life.

This might not be our usual posture of heart, but it is true. And because it is true, we now have a decision to make. And it is one of the most important spiritual decisions you or I can ever make. When we look at our lives and all the stuff that is in them, we have to decide how we are going to see them.

One way to see your life is this: your waking moments are mostly filled with a bunch of stuff that keeps you from knowing God. If you see your life this way, you will likely spend a lot of time blaming the world around you—including the people around you—and viewing nearly everything as an obstacle to your spiritual growth.

This is certainly one way to view the world, but it is not good. Seeing the world this way can make you only angry or lazy. You will eventually come up against circumstances or people who are exceptionally difficult and, by their very existence in your life, make prayer (and nearly every other attempt at spiritual growth) exceedingly difficult, too. If you're prone to anger, you will rail against these circumstances or people—*I would be so much godlier if it weren't for you!* Or if you're prone to laziness, you will retreat and relent—*There's nothing I can do about this so I guess I will strop trying to be godly.*

Many of us think like this. I view my life and all that is in it like this far too often to comfortably admit.

But there is another way to see our lives. One of my favorite truths in the Bible comes from Psalm 24. The author, David, states very simply, "The earth is the Lord's and the fullness thereof" (v. 1). If that's true, then it changes everything. Especially how we should see the "distractions" of our lives.

My daughter crying in the middle of the night because her teeth are cutting through her tender, two-year-old gums? That belongs to the Lord.

My son banging on the bathroom door while I try to pray in the shower? That belongs to the Lord.

My ever-growing to-do list and all the responsibilities that I face with my job? That belongs to the Lord.

The traffic that is making me late for dinner? That belongs to the Lord.

My tired, aching body that is sleep-deprived and honestly is in no mood to pray right now? That belongs to the Lord.

My anxious, worried heart that can't slow down enough to think about God, let alone have a meaningful conversation with him right now? Yes. Even that belongs to the Lord.

My weakness in prayer won't be solved by removing the distractions I face. I will still be the same person. I will still find ways to avoid God. I will still find ways to blame others. I will still find ways to be angry and lazy. Because I am, at my core, weak and self-centered and frail, regardless of my context. While it's tempting to think otherwise, it simply is not true.

What I need, then, is not some magical way to remove myself from distractions. What I need is to become the kind of person who can see God in every distraction. Let me say that again: *What I need is to become the kind of person who can see God in every distraction.* To find out what he wants to say to me through the life he is giving me, and all the stuff that comes with that.

And then I need to pray.

If prayer is anything, it is first and foremost God's thing. I don't know why God gives—or at least allows—so many distracting circumstances and people to persist in our lives. But he does. I can only trust that he has his reasons. What I do know is that every external distraction I face throughout my day is his hidden invitation to come to him.

And these invitations are sometimes *very* hidden. Let's take the simple task of mowing the lawn. It's probably something I need to talk to someone about because I *hate* it with an irrational amount of emotion. I would rather get a cavity filled, and then have the dentist drill out the cavity he just filled and fill it again, but this time without the numbing agent, than mow the lawn.

One time, however, I didn't hate mowing the lawn. In fact, this particular experience is still one of the most remarkable moments in my spiritual journey I have ever had. During a day off, I started up my push mower and began to mow. There I was, with full hatred heating up my heart toward the job in front of me, and something began to happen. I started to pray. As I opened my heart to God, all I can say is that I experienced something so unexpected and, quite honestly, a little embarrassing that I'm hesitant to even try to put it into words. But here goes:

In the middle of my front lawn, pushing a mower, sweating, I felt the God of the universe in such a powerful way that I had to hide my face and simply stand still in front of him. I felt an amazing amount of gratitude for things, for *everything*. Things seemed to slow down and become very still. And I knew that I was not alone. I started to cry. Which is weird for me because I don't often cry and I most definitely do not cry alone on my front lawn in the middle of a summer afternoon.

I'm sure that whoever drove by and saw me standing in my yard, eyes closed, with a running lawn mower that I wasn't even pushing, felt a little uncomfortable. *I* felt a little uncomfortable. But God's love for me at that moment was far greater than any awkwardness I was feeling. And I wasn't about to move away from the experience too soon.

That day is still full of meaning for me, years later. I thought mowing the lawn was an empty distraction in my attempt to live a spiritual life. God graciously reminded me that nothing is empty. He can fill anything with his love and power in an instant.

It is a lot to think about when we start to realize this, but we have something greater than thoughts. We have a *comfort*. To have access to a God who can enter into any moment—even if he's not invited—and fill it with love, power, and his purpose means that we are never outside his reach. We are never far away from the possibility of great significance and meaning. The places in our lives where we feel the most bored, the most insignificant, the most distracted—even these places are opportunities to find God.

God, you are speaking to me right now. Maybe not through actual words, but you are speaking. Help me to hear what you want me to hear through this situation, this person that I want to view as a distraction from you. What's in front of me right now belongs to you. And you want me to use whatever that is in front of me as a way to connect with you. Help me.

That's a pretty good prayer right there. Maybe one of the best we can pray. Especially in the face of our "distractions."

4 GUILT

IN THE SECOND chapter of this book, I wrote about how guilt is often a motivator for our prayers. I want to press that a bit further, because I know that one of the most dominant emotions we feel throughout our lives is guilt. It's worth a deeper look.

One of Christianity's greatest heroes has a name that few can confidently pronounce. Is it "*Au*-gust-ine" like the month or "A-*gus*-tine" like the pudgy mouse in *Cinderella*? Regardless of how you pronounce his name, Saint Augustine influenced our understandings of God and the world in profound ways. You would be hard-pressed to find five other individuals who have had the scope of influence that he had and continues to have today.

Augustine (say it however you want to) wrote about a lot of things. This is a massive understatement, actually. He wrote more than *five million words*. And that's just what has survived into our modern day. We can safely assume that he wrote even more. Which is remarkable, given that he lived in the 300s AD and didn't have the technological advantages that we have today to make writing easier.

Beyond his impact on Christian doctrine and theology, Augustine is perhaps most famous for something that we wouldn't necessarily expect him to be—pears. He records the story in his famous autobiography *Confessions*, and it goes like this: When Augustine was a teenager, he did what most teenage boys do—he got into trouble with his friends. One night he and his fellow hooligans snuck into a nearby orchard and stole a bunch of pears. After committing this scandalous act, Augustine was hit by a question that he couldn't shake: *Why did I steal the pears?* He searched his heart for a meaningful explanation, but instead found none. He wasn't hungry. And he didn't particularly like pears, certainly no more so than any other fruit. So why did he do something morally wrong if it didn't provide him with something he needed—for example, nourishment? And it didn't provide him with something he enjoyed—for example, pleasure. In a great display of irony, Augustine didn't even eat the stolen fruit. He tossed the pears away and instead retreated to solitude to sift through the structures of his own heart.

We might not be able to relate to this kind of scrupulous examination today, but for the teenage Augustine, these pears created an anxiety that sank him into an earthquake of the soul. Through this simple and relatively benign act of stealing the pears, Augustine prodded the depths of the human heart—*his* human heart. He ended up asking one of the most important questions that any of us can ask, and that most of us can't answer: *Why do we do the things we do, especially the bad things?*

The answer he found isn't encouraging. Augustine, having removed himself from his friends and the pears, concluded that the only reason he stole the pears was that his heart simply *enjoyed* doing something wrong. This realization unsettled his foundation.

What kind of a person does something wrong for the simple enjoyment of doing wrong things?

Augustine couldn't escape it. And so began his despair.

Augustine recorded this event in *Confessions*. It's a long book and I can say that I've read it only once. I can't say that I remember a lot of what he wrote. But what I do remember, and what people far smarter than I would say is worth remembering, is that Augustine encountered more than a collapse of his morals the night he stole the pears. He encountered a collapse of innocence. He encountered a collapse of his understanding of his ability to be good.

We have all had this same encounter, even if pears aren't directly involved. At some point in our lives, we come face-to-face with our own inability to live the kind of life that we feel we should live. Maybe we steal something, or say something hurtful to someone, or actually hurt someone physically. Maybe we lust for something that isn't ours. Maybe we tell a lie. The point is that we do something that almost immediately brings a sense of darkness into our hearts. We feel guilt and shame and maybe even conviction for what we've thought or said or done. And then we usually feel a second wave of guilt and shame and maybe even panic because we realize that the wrong thing we have just said or thought or done can't be taken back. We can't un-think that judgmental thought. We can't un-say those hurtful words. We can't un-steal the pears.

I don't know much about biology or physiology, but I am

amazed by what I do know. Take, for example, our human bodies. Let's say you are cutting up some carrots for a salad. You have a sharp knife and a cutting board and you start your cutting with no problems. But then you lose focus—just for a second, maybe even a millisecond—and suddenly you feel a sharp pain in one of your fingers and the little slices of carrots are now covered in blood. You mutter some words you wouldn't say in front of your mother, put the knife down, and start your triage. Cold water. Wet paper towels. Periodically pulling the wad of paper towel back several times to see if the bleeding has stopped. Finally it stops. You put a Band-Aid on it and go back to making lunch again. This time you choose soup from a can instead of a salad, because you don't have to cut soup. The safer choice.

You may feel some stiffness in your finger for a few days afterward, but the amazing thing—the truly amazing thing, in my opinion—is that in a few weeks, your finger is healed. The gash is gone. No more leaking blood. No more annoying scab. Back to normal.

Our bodies trick us. From a very early age, they tell us that things can be fixed. Things will go back to normal. Of course, I'm not talking about losing a limb or undergoing a major surgery or suffering a major, life-altering disease. There are things we face, even from an early age, that cannot be undone. But for the most part, and for most people, we grow up with the expectation that everything can be fixed.

When Augustine stole the pears, I think he realized—maybe for the first time—that not everything can be fixed. And more important, that *he* couldn't fix everything. He lived in a world with consequences, and those consequences, once set in motion, were like a growing wave that only had the ability to keep moving forward until it finally crashed onto the shore of his own conscience. He couldn't go back in time and make a different decision. The *right* decision. He had to face the fact that he had done something wrong. And even more difficult, he had to go on living in the wake of his wrongness.

This is a really hard thing to face, for any of us. Not to be able to heal our lives from the wrong things that we have done drives us to all kinds of feelings and actions. When you read *Confessions*, you see that Augustine distills these feelings and actions into a primary sensation, again something that he cannot shake and doesn't have an answer for: *guilt*.

Now we see that the pears aren't the point—for either Augustine or for us. The point is that every single one of us underperforms. We cannot live the way we want to live, and certainly not in the way that others want us to live. This goes even deeper when we start to talk about God, because one of the realities we also live within, whether we are Christians or not, is that there is a cosmic communication of right and wrong that reaches every human heart. And we are very often on the wrong side of it.

Therapists, counselors, psychologists, pastors, priests, and even artists across disciplines and faith traditions debate the healthiness and even usefulness of this feeling of guilt, but what isn't debated—at least, I haven't seen it debated—is its existence in every human heart. We all feel guilty.

This starts Augustine toward his conversion. It's a beautiful story and worth your time to read, even if it's just the condensed version. As Augustine encounters salvation and mercy and grace and all the good things that God gives him (and us), he also encounters something that shepherds his heart in a tangible way. He finds *rest*.

For Augustine, one of the symptoms of a guilty heart is an inner restlessness or anxiety that plays in the background of his life, regardless of the circumstances. It's like a low-grade fever or a ringing of the ears. It's always there. And it affects everything. This inner restlessness leads to worry, frustration, pain, sorrow, indulgence. It also leads to more guilt, more shame, more unsteadiness.

When Augustine meets God, he experiences relief from this restlessness. Not complete relief, but complete enough. Meaning, he tastes something good and rearranges the trajectory of his life and soul to point toward this goodness. As he takes steps toward this goodness, more relief comes. He finds his inner restlessness less of an issue than what it used to be.

He famously sums up this journey with this thought: *Thou hast made us for thyself, O Lord, and our heart is restless until it finds its rest in thee.*[1]

Doesn't this sound *wonderful?* To know that we were made with purpose, made with a home in mind, and made by a God who has the answer for our guilt-inspired restlessness of heart?

This is what I need to remember as I pray.

Like Augustine, I can't shake the fact that I do wrong things for no other reason or satisfaction besides the fact that there is something inside me that simply enjoys doing them. This is a horrible thing to admit. Even more horrible to face. But it's true. And I can't help but feel an immense amount of guilt because of how true it is.

When I try to pray, I wish I could say that I bring pure motives and a free heart into that space. Sometimes I get closer than others, but for the most part, I come into the space of prayer with an inner restlessness. This restlessness stems from a lot of seeds, but the primary one is guilt. I feel guilty for spending hours of my day feeling slighted and resentful toward the people around me. I feel guilty for not being a better husband. I feel guilty for not being a better dad. I feel guilty for sleeping in instead of getting up early to read the Bible. I feel guilty for spending so much of my money on myself. I feel guilty for calling my mom those names when I was twelve. I feel guilty for not being a better Christian. I feel guilty for feeling so guilty and not living in the freedom that Jesus says he gives to me.

All of this guilt leaves me feeling anxious, restless. Is God going to hear me today? Or is he going to shut me out until I figure out a better way to deal with all of my issues? Is he going to be kind and gracious and merciful?

Restlessness.

I try to remember Jesus' own words to people like me:

Are you tired? Worn out? Burned out on religion? Come to me. Get away with me and you'll recover your life. I'll show you how to take a real rest. Walk with me and work with me—watch how I do it. Learn the unforced rhythms of grace. I won't lay anything heavy or ill-fitting on you. Keep company with me and you'll learn to live freely and lightly. (Matthew 11:28–30 MSG)

It works for a minute or two, but then I'm back where I was. Feeling guilty that they didn't work for longer.

Guilt, experts would say, makes relationships so difficult because it cuts two ways. First, guilt tells you that you aren't good enough to be loved. Second, guilt tells you that you can't trust anyone who shows you love because, remember, you aren't good enough to be loved.

These two cuts are catastrophically damaging to a satisfying prayer life. God is love, and creates a relationship with us based on love. Even if we know this to be true from a rational, theological place, our restless hearts have trouble experiencing this truth. It too often runs too cold. Our incessant guilt and restless hearts prevent us from surrendering to his love. We simply cannot believe, let alone accept, that Love loves us— fully, truly, without conditions.

So when we try to pray, we start from two rungs down. If prayer is, in its simplest form, a friendship founded upon God's love for us, our guilt-laden restless hearts sabotage us from the beginning because we don't see ourselves as worthy of love at all. Deeper still, if we have even a marginal understanding of God's love, we know that it is the purest love that exists, that could ever exist. This initially sounds like a good thing. But if you don't see yourself as lovable because of your constant underperformance, accepting this kind of love can sometimes feel impossible. We feel like the homely overweight prom date who has to sit next to the gorgeous cheerleader. Ugly. And made uglier by the company we are keeping.

Christians throughout the centuries have talked about prayer through a common image of a beggar looking for bread.

The beggar has empty hands and wants someone to fill them. God is the One who can and does fill them. I think this is a really helpful image that I have used often in my attempts at prayer. Mostly because I often feel like a beggar, and mostly because I think this image gets at what it means to be in relationship with God. I am empty. He has what leads to my fullness. And more than that, he wants to give fullness to me. My part in this whole thing is to ask and then to receive whatever he wants to give to me.

I believe this. All of this. With my whole heart.

And this is one of the main reasons why I fail to make more progress with my prayers. And it's probably the same issue for you, as well. While God is a perfect giver, I'm not a perfect receiver. When I come to him with all of my requests, all of my fears, all of my worries, he is more than able to handle all of these—and more. But with the same hands that I use to bring myself to him, I also refuse to receive what he could give to me because, at the bottom of my gut, I don't believe that I am lovable. I've done too much. And I can't fix it. How could God love *me?*

On the rare occasions that his love breaks through my guilt and I can receive it in freedom and purity of heart, those moments don't last like I want them to. Because something inevitably happens that steals my trust in him. Maybe I have a hard day at work or a conflict at home or my bank account runs low and suddenly I think back to what a horrible person I am and how there is no way that I could trust that God loves me, and these circumstances are proof that my mistrust is well founded.

The two cuts of guilt wound any chance I have of entering into a conversation based on love because I don't see myself as lovable and I don't trust someone who says otherwise.

I wouldn't have ever wanted to be a Puritan, but here they help me. Despite their reputation for strict and rigid doctrine, they actually cared about the dynamics of experiencing God a lot more than they are given credit for. Plagued by the same sense of guilt and restlessness that Augustine experienced, and that I experience, too, Puritan pastors and writers talked often about how beliefs should lead us to worship. The more we understand who God is and what he has done, the more we should be moved to surrender to him and his lordship over our lives—the head and the heart working together to move us toward a greater, deeper love for Love Himself.

I think this is why we read the Bible, especially the New Testament, and see the same few messages written over and over. God loves us. He forgives us. He wants to spend eternity with us. He created us to experience all of these things and, through Jesus, enables this kind of reality to drop into our hearts and change the way we see the world around us. None of this is particularly complicated.

But we don't believe these things, do we? Why not? John, another father of our Christian faith, sums it all up: *our hearts condemn us* (1 John 3:20).

So what do we do with condemning hearts? How do we change what we believe about ourselves?

We have to look repeatedly at the truth about who God is, even if we don't believe it. Even if we don't trust in God's love, we have to continually put it before us through things like reading the Bible, singing songs of worship about him, gathering with other Christians, even praying. In some ways, we have to "go through the motions" a bit. This isn't faking anything because we are still being honest about the true condition of our hearts. We aren't pretending that things are "fine." We are honest about our coldness toward holy things. But still we press on. Like a beggar looking for bread. Admitting our hunger. Admitting our fatigue. Admitting our weakness. But still searching for food because that's the only thing that will help us. And to give up the search is to give up on finding the very thing that we need the most.

When I put myself in front of the truths about God and his ways, even when I don't feel like it, I am putting myself in the position of light. Hang around light long enough, get close enough to light, and you will eventually feel warmth. And warmth is what we really need.

This is where prayer becomes less about my guilt and my inability to believe in the God I'm looking toward and more about God supernaturally overcoming my condemning heart. I don't pretend to understand how this works. That kind of truth is reserved for people far more spiritual than I am. But what I can say is that I have had precious few times where I bend my knee and heart in prayer, and before I even realize what's going on, I actually believe that God loves me. He's not disapproving of me. And he has zero expectations that I should be able to fix what's wrong with me. The light of this truth about who he is and what he thinks about me becomes something warm that fills my heart and overcomes my sense of guilt and mistrust.

It's in these moments that prayer becomes what I always hoped it could be—nearness to God. Warmth showing itself through friendship. Or maybe it's friendship showing itself through warmth. Either way it feels far better than guilt.

5 GRATITUDE

FOR MOST OF us, when we think about prayer, we think about speaking to God. Or at the very least, thinking words toward God. This is a good and helpful way to think about prayer because our hearts have a lot to say. To know that we have a place where we are heard is one of the most important comforts we can have as human beings.

But what are we *supposed* to say?

Where do we even begin?

Genesis makes a lot of sense, and not just because it opens with the pregnant line "In the beginning…" So much of what we need to believe comes from Genesis, specifically the first three chapters. If I had only three chapters of the entire Old Testament to explain God, the world, and my place within it, these would be it. I wouldn't need anything else.

Within these three chapters, we see several things that can help us with our prayers. The story goes like this: Before there was anything, there was God. I know it's hard to think this way, but imagine that nothing existed. No sky. No earth. No space. No stars. No sun. No anything. Just this mysterious, creative, divine Person. And each of these characteristics is important to remember. Mysterious—there's a lot about this Person that we don't know. Creative—something about this Person likes to make stuff. Divine—this Person possesses qualities and attributes that make him sit above everything else.

Out of his mystery and creativity and divinity, this Person causes what was previously nonexistent to exist. The Latin word for this kind of productivity is *ex nihilo*, which loosely means that God didn't create his stuff from other stuff that was lying around, but rather everything he created came out of nothing. He is not just a really gifted assembler of things. He's not MacGyver. He's the kind of person who, out of nothing, has the mysterious, creative, divine power to make something. Actually, a lot of somethings.

The book of Genesis shows us another curious observation. This creative God makes things by speaking them into existence, by his words. Which is another way to say that God makes things like the sky and the stars and the planets and the moon, simply by his power and authority. Whatever he says comes into being. He speaks, and then things like the earth and water and plants and animals appear. He makes colors and flavors and storms and other beautiful things that put his power and goodness on display, all through his spoken words.

And he also makes human beings. The way that he makes human beings, and the exact time that he takes to make them, is shrouded in mystery. There are many people who get caught up in trying to delineate an accurate timeline of creation and human existence from these three chapters in Genesis, but I think that misses the point. God is not a cosmic Julia Child giving us a biological recipe for human life here. Instead, he is like the artist who gives us a beautiful representation—an essence—of his intentions for creating in the first place. He is a God who makes stuff. And that "stuff" includes men and women who have a unique capacity to appreciate his creation in ways that the entire rest of his creation doesn't.

In addition to this capacity to appreciate God and his creation, God also gives humans the ability to understand him. Another way to think about this is the idea of *relationship*. One of the most powerful images that surfaces from these first three chapters is this mysterious, creative, divine Person interacting with Adam and Eve—the first man and woman—on a *personal* level. He talks with them. He walks with them, which is a sign of friendship. He anticipates their needs—"It isn't good that Adam is alone. I'll make him another human being to be in relationship with." And he gives them gifts. Tremendous gifts like fruit and shade and rain and sunrises marked with beauty. He gives them the gift of nakedness, which doesn't initially sound like a gift (or maybe it does), but it actually is. Most of our lives are spent pretending and hiding. Imagine living with such confidence and clear identity that you are entirely comfortable walking around in your own skin and nothing else. And no one judges you or shames you or excludes you from anything because of who you are. If that's not a gift, I don't know what is.

One of the main ideas that God tries to tell us through these three chapters in Genesis is that he is *good*. He doesn't *have* to do any of this. He didn't have to create at all. Or he could have created a world that was miserable and hard and empty of anything good. But he didn't. The fact that he made human beings to experience a relationship with him at all is a sign that God is into luxury. He didn't need to do that. And he certainly didn't need to make food taste good, the sky display beautiful colors, the shade of a tree provide rest and relief from the sun, the puppy look so cute and playful. Something about God's creative process should give us pause. It certainly seems like he went above and beyond.

Part of God's goodness also comes through his restrictions. I am not an artist, but I do love art. Or more accurately, I love beautiful things. When I was in high school, I remember that I had to take an art class. Our teacher helped us learn how to paint, draw, and sculpt. I didn't enjoy this last one, as I seem to have been born with an aversion to the feeling of clay. In any case, our teacher assigned us a project in which we had to make a clay fish. It had to be big and round and then we had to paint it. I don't remember anything specific about my fish except that I really struggled with its lips. *What kind of lips do fish have?* I didn't know. And our teacher honored my "creative process" by refusing to tell me. So what I remember is that there I was, making this clay fish with strange lips, muttering under my breath about the absurdity of the whole thing. As soon as my sculpture came out of the kiln, I thought hard about how I could "accidentally" drop it and just take the *F.* It was horrendous.

But it was *mine. My* work.

Something about the creative process put my ability to choose—or not choose—on display. As the artist (and I use that term loosely), I held a certain amount of power and control over my artistic creation. I made the decision to color my fish green. I made the decision to etch in some eyelashes. I made the decision not to scrap it altogether or intentionally destroy it upon its emergence from the kiln.

God is the same way. He is the ultimate creator. And he stands in a place of power and control over all that he has created. All of this means that he can do whatever he wants to with his creations. He gets to decide what they look like, how they act, how they are supposed to function. Because he is good and everything he does is good.

I'm not trying to get into a long discussion about God's goodness and how it relates to the pain and sorrow we experience, sometimes daily, in our lives. That would be too long of an exploration here, but the quick answer is all of that is in the first three chapters of Genesis, as well. For our purposes in regard to prayer, however, the point is that if we believe that God is good and that all he does is good, we have to also believe that he is being good to us even when he tells us "no."

One of the "no's" that God gave Adam and Eve had to do with a certain tree. When God created the earth, he created a part of that earth in the form of a garden. We don't know a lot about this garden, but it must have been magnificent. Teeming with trees and fruit and flowers and animals and beauty and life in its fullest, most satisfying forms. Within this garden, God made one tree that he said was "off-limits." This tree had something to do with knowledge in its truest, deepest form. If human beings ate the fruit of this tree, they would somehow experience a level of awareness, specifically about the nature of good and evil, that would ruin them.

No one knows why God made this tree in the first place. Anyone who says they do is either woefully naïve or woefully arrogant about their place in the world. The origin of evil is the black box of history and we simply have no idea where, when, and why it even existed in the first place. But it is there. And it has been there since the beginning of our existence.

Back to the garden and the forbidden tree.

God, out of his goodness, gives his first humans a restriction. He says that they can enjoy any fruit from any tree except this particular one. Most of us are familiar with the rest of the story. A serpent comes—again, from where we don't know— who whispers temptations into Eve's ear.

Did God really say that you would die if you ate this forbidden fruit?

What is this word die? *You've never experienced it before, have you?*

Perhaps to "die" is a good thing?

You've experienced only goodness so far. Why would this be any different?

Perhaps God is withholding from you?

Perhaps he isn't as good as he says he is?

What if you just took a little taste to see what happens?

God isn't here, is he?

Trust me.

The next thing we see in the story is Adam and Eve ignoring God's restriction, casting off his command, and indulging their appetite for curiosity with the forbidden fruit. Jews and Christians throughout history point to this episode as the first sin. Behind the eating of the fruit, they say, lies the real sin of pride. Adam and Eve simultaneously ignored God, listened to someone who wasn't God, and assumed the place of God by deciding what was right and wrong for their lives—which all stemmed from an inner pride. They revolted against God, forsook his goodness, and doubted his ability to sit in a place of authority over their lives.

I certainly agree with all of this. Pride was the first sin. If Adam and Eve hadn't acted out of their elevated desires to be like God—which is one of the best definitions of pride—and felt like they were entitled to something more than what they had, we wouldn't be in this mess of broken and wounded humanity that we are in today. Pride affects us all and sits behind every other sin that we commit.

But I also think there was more going on in Adam and Eve's hearts than just pride.

Pause and think again about *where* they were. Think about the most beautiful place you have ever seen. Think about the most amazing meal you have ever eaten. Think about the safest you have ever felt. Think about the freest you have ever been.

This had to be what the garden felt like. Every physical, emotional, relational, and spiritual need met. And not just met, but *lavishly* met. Beyond having their needs met, Adam and Eve had something greater than this, too. They had God himself. They had direct, unfiltered access to God himself.

We simply cannot fully understand what this would have been like to experience this kind of reality. Beauty and intimacy and a feeling of satisfaction beyond words.

Which leads me to this: Beyond pride, Adam and Eve also had to have had feelings of ingratitude in their hearts, as well.

When they ate the forbidden fruit, they shifted their eyes away from all the goodness that existed around them and instead focused on the perceived "goodness" that they didn't have. This is the definition of ingratitude. To ignore what you have while at the same time feeling like something is missing from your life because of what you don't have.

A man named Ignatius (not of Antioch, but of Loyola), a Spanish priest and theologian who lived in the sixteenth century, was keen on this point. In one of his letters, he wrote that ingratitude is the "cause, beginning, and origin of all evils and sins."[1] What I think Ignatius means is that sin is defined by wanting something you don't have. For example, we steal because we want money or some other thing of value that we don't have. We worry because we don't have control over the future. We lust for someone else's body because we don't have permission to enjoy it. We covet because we don't have what someone else already has, and we think that we would be happier if we had it and they didn't.

The list could go on. But the point is this: we commit sins out of our perceived position of lack. And we falsely believe that if we could somehow obtain what we don't have, but want, then we would feel complete and even happy. In short, we are ungrateful for the things that God has put around our lives and we feel like we deserve something more.

And this is Ignatius' point. That each of our sins comes from a place of displeasure with God's provision for our lives. Even though we live in this amazing garden—that we didn't create and don't deserve—we want *more*. Instead of staying low and humble in gratitude, we rise up in pride and ingratitude, shake our fists at God, and tell him, "You haven't done enough for me so I'm going to take things into my own hands and get what I want, what I deserve!"

Ingratitude, the sister sin to pride, is far subtler, yet just as dangerous to our souls. When we forget about all the good things that God has put around us, we buy into the lie that getting more than what we have will leave us in a position of contentment, which never works out to be true.

So what does all of this have to do with prayer?

Good prayer begins with gratitude. An awareness of all the ways that God has been good to you in the past and is being good to you right now. When we struggle to know what we should say to God, gratitude is probably the best place to begin:

These legs and lungs work.
Thank you.
This heart can feel love and warmth.
Thank you.
These eyes can take in beauty.
Thank you.
Things are not as bad as they could be.
Thank you.
Thing are better than I deserve them to be.
Thank you.

I never played football growing up, but I am familiar with the clichéd scene of someone tackling someone else and leaving him unconscious. Half of the crowd cheers while the other half gasps. A group of coaches rush out to the field to see if the unmoving pile of a man is okay. I don't know if this is what still happens, but it used to be that a medical professional would join the coaches and, in an effort to revive the knocked-out player, would shove smelling salts up into his nose. I have never smelled these salts, but apparently they are so pungent and strong that they kick the player's brain back into consciousness and he is ready to go for the next play.

This is a little like what gratitude does for us. Life is hard. Really hard, in fact. On top of that, our lives are typically too busy. This combination of difficulty and overcrowdedness runs our souls over and leaves us in a daze. We have trouble responding to God in the ways that we would like to. Not because we don't care about him or don't want to know him better, but because we are simply tired. It feels like too much work to lift up our souls in an effort to connect with the God we know we need. So there we stay, heaped into a barely moving pile, feeling run over and disoriented, wondering where we are in the world and how we got there.

I am sympathetic to this state. I have been and continue to be there often. When I'm feeling this way, it's easy for me to compound my condition of fatigue by adding on top of that guilt and shame—*I should be doing more to care for my soul... I should read the Bible...I should pray more...I should pray longer...I can't believe I slept in again...I can't believe I'd rather binge-watch a show than retreat to my room and pray.*

None of this works to motivate me toward anything that resembles health and intimacy and life with God. None of it. When I see God and my relationship to him as chiefly defined by what I *should* be doing, I only add to the already deep awareness that I do not possess whatever is needed to generate or sustain the kind of life with God that I want, that I feel compelled to seek. So I feel like the sprinter who puts his feet in the blocks, takes his position, but when the gun goes off, lies down and quits before he even takes a step because he knows that he can't possibly complete the race.

How do you get your legs to run when you feel like they don't work?

How do you get your soul to open up to God when you feel like it doesn't work?

This isn't a new phenomenon. Paul, one of history's greatest followers of God, wrote quite often about how to find God in the midst of trials. One of his most helpful writings comes to us through a letter he wrote to a group of believers in Philippi. In this letter, Paul writes that Christians are called to rejoice, regardless of what they are facing. Paul, knowing just how fragile the human heart is, repeats himself, saying, "Again, I say 'Rejoice!'" (Philippians 4:4).

This is even more moving when we pull back and view Paul's life. He was beaten. Stoned. Left for dead. Shipwrecked. And then, after the shipwreck, he found himself on an island. While warming himself by a fire, a snake came out from who knows where and bit him on the hand.

And the list goes on. He was persecuted, falsely accused, and jailed. He felt loneliness and pain. At one point he wrote to his friend and asked for his coat. Apparently, one of the greatest Christians in the history of the world was tired of being cold.

Through all of these trying experiences—and we can only assume many, many more that he left out of his writings—Paul was able to somehow still experience a nearness with God that most of us would envy. When we read through the writings that we have of his, we see many things. But one of the most central themes is a sense of genuine gratitude that grows from his understanding of Jesus and his work.

This is how Paul can admonish his readers—including us today—to rejoice. And then to rejoice again. Despite his sufferings, despite his times of doubt and spiritual dryness, Paul found joy. He found an ability to look past the cloudiness of his pain and despair and push through to a real, deep, living trust in God. Gratitude played a central role in his ability to do this because you can't rejoice without being grateful. It's impossible.

As Ignatius points out, ingratitude grows along with our pride when we think that someone is withholding things from us. We think that we deserve more than we have. We feel entitled. We wonder what our lives would be like—how much *better* our lives would be—if we could experience some type of perceived goodness that we aren't currently able to experience. What can happen, then, is that we fixate our emotions and energies on what we don't have instead of what we do have. And the dangerous condition that results is discontentment. Like spokes from a hub, self-pity usually follows discontentment, which is then followed by bitterness and resentment and anger and, ultimately, despair. This cluster of emotions moves our hearts away from God and has near-catastrophic implications for intimacy with him. Mainly this one: *how can you trust someone that you suspiciously think is withholding from you?*

Once this domino falls—this loss of trust—it's hard to enter into any kind of real prayer with God. Sure, we might make known our desires, apologize for a few things, ask God to fix some of the situations around us. But this methodology of working through list-like requests leaves us wanting because it works too much around a center of what we don't currently have. To be sure, God wants us to tell him about what we want from him. But if that's the center of our relationship with him, we're in trouble. Prayer like this becomes transactional, like going to a bank counter and asking for a withdrawal. When was the last time you ever felt intimacy at a bank counter?

Gratitude helps us know what to say to God because it gives our relationship with him a center of trust. When we practice gratitude, we take our eyes off what we don't have and put them on what we do have. Or more accurately, what we have been *given*. We look at our lives and all that they include and we find things to be grateful for. This may take a lot of work at times because life is seasonal. Everyone experiences seasons in which there seems to be more pain than goodness. But goodness is still there. If you're alive and breathing, you've been given a gift. And everything beyond that—the sun you feel on your face, the smile you see in a stranger, the guacamole you eat at your lunch, the laughter you share with your friend—are gifts piled on top of gifts.

None of this is easy. Especially for those of us with more critical, pessimistic dispositions. It's far easier to focus on what we don't have than on what we do. But the fight for gratitude is worth it. And my experience has been that when I start to speak to God about what I'm grateful for, it's like a snowflake that starts an avalanche. The more I practice gratitude, the more aware I become of things to be grateful for. The more I notice the gifts that God has given to me in the past and is giving me right now, the more my heart feels trained to notice the kind of God he is—a God who loves to give to his kids, including me. Everything he withholds is for his own good reasons. He doesn't keep things from me because he's cruel or stingy or, even worse, unable to give me what he wants to. All of his withholdings come from a place of wisdom, and even mercy.

None of this changes the places in my prayers where I voice what I want. I still feel a lot of lack at times. I still long for things to be better. I still long to be happy. And I tell God all of this. But if I am able to show gratitude first, the longings are different. They feel, somehow, *cleaner*. Free from my self-pity and bitterness and left-out-ness. They feel pure. And I emerge from my times of prayer trusting God more than when I entered, because my longings grow from a place of gratitude for what I already have, not discontentment for what I don't.

> Rejoice in the Lord always; again I will say, rejoice. Let your reasonableness be known to everyone. The Lord is at hand; do not be anxious about anything, but in everything by prayer and supplication with thanksgiving let your requests be made known to God. And the peace of God, which surpasses all understanding, will guard your hearts and your minds in Christ Jesus. (Philippians 4:4–7)

6 DISAPPOINTMENT

ONE OF THE hardest things about prayer is the inherent disappointment it often includes. We ask for things. Sometimes we get them. Most of the time we don't. And even when we do get what we ask for, it usually takes much longer than we expected. Or it comes wrapped in different paper. Or it comes in a different form entirely. And we don't always know what to do with it.

This is also one of the things that makes prayer so exhausting at times—this repeated cycle of emotions and faith and soul-baring that risks the hope of having a request answered, even in the face of repeated denials. To be sure, we have our private lists of victories. But we also carry into the space of prayer another, often longer list of defeats. That time we asked for God to heal our relative or friend and he didn't. That time we asked God to make our relationship with our spouse better and he didn't. That time we asked for God to give us a job—*now*—and he didn't. To put ourselves into a position of vulnerability by exposing our desires to a powerful God, and then to hear or receive nothing, and then to be told that we should *keep trusting* this same God again and again creates a belief-fatigue in our hearts.

Am I foolish for again trusting in this God who did nothing for me the last time I asked him to do something?

Is he even real?

Does he even care?

Or worse, he is real, he does care, but he is unable to do anything about my life right now.

A few years ago, my wife and one of her best friends boarded a plane and left our gray February skies to go to Florida for a long weekend. We had three kids at the time, ages six-and-a-half down to two, which meant that my wife had essentially been pregnant, giving birth, recovering from giving birth, or nursing a child for the previous seven years. One of the things that no one tells you about having babies—maybe they do but we just refuse to hear it—is how much freedom you lose. And by "you," I mainly mean the mothers. This trip to Florida was a small way for her to reclaim some of that freedom.

The trip to Florida was also a small way to test my parenting capabilities. With Mom out of the house (out of the state!) for four days, that meant that I had our three kids all to myself. I was responsible for every meal, every shower, every ride to school, every diaper change and bottom wipe. It truly is a miracle that I'm typing this today.

On one of the days, I was spent. My five-year-old son stomped down the hall around six in the morning to wake me up, and so began the day. I made breakfast, played, made lunch, played some more, put our youngest down for a nap, played some more, and then played some more. Somehow I got a shower in the midst of all the playing. I'm not saying this for sympathy because I realize that stay-at-home moms do this routine *every day*. I'm just pointing out that I had only five minutes to myself the entire day. And even that was interrupted by my son, informing me that he didn't like the show I had put on the TV for all three of them to watch.

By 4 p.m., I needed to check out a bit. I'm not proud of this, but there are a lot of things I'm not proud of in my life and this feels like one I can share. So in my shame, I set up some toys on our living room floor for our two youngest kids, gave a book to our oldest, and decided to have some personal time before dinner. Which was, of course, and expectedly, interrupted. Despite the interruptions, I managed to find a few minutes to watch one of my favorite cooking shows.

I love to watch cooking shows. I am not a good cook, but I love—genuinely *love*—to eat good food. There is something about someone who is skilled in selecting ingredients and matching tastes and textures and flavor profiles together, and then arranging their creations in a beautiful way, that moves me. I know that sounds strange to some, but think about it: What other kind of art can you enjoy in such intimate ways? What other kind of beauty can you see, touch, and then taste? A well-prepared meal hits so many of my senses. It nourishes me. In both body and soul.

My kids also love to eat good food. But their definition of "good" varies from mine. While they are fairly adventurous and appreciative eaters—especially for their age—they still, like most kids, possess a simpler palate. On this night, they asked for one of their favorites: macaroni and cheese (from a box), hot dogs (from a sealed plastic bag), and applesauce (from a foil-lidded plastic cup).

I am a dad, which means that I want to give my kids the world. If macaroni and cheese and hot dogs and applesauce are what they want, I want to give that to them. Being a dad also means that I am practical and maybe even a bit lazy. I'm not about to make myself a different meal than what I'm making the kids.

So there I am standing in our kitchen, pouring the powdered cheese (pause and really think about this for a minute—cheese that has been so overly processed that it has turned into *powder*) into a pot full of boiled pasta and butter and milk. It's orange. So orange that it occurs to me that no cheese in the world actually looks like this. I think it might even be radioactive at one point because, for a brief moment, it appears to glow. In the midst of calculating the half-life of a cheese isotope, I'm also cutting up these thin cylinders of processed meat, which is supposedly kosher, into little pieces and arranging them next to some ketchup. And then I'm peeling off the foil lids of individual plastic cups of sauced apples, which is supposedly all-natural, and placing them on the plate, next to the cut-up hot dogs, the ketchup, and the mounds of glowing macaroni.

But I can still see the TV from our kitchen. On the screen I see a chef from Peru hiking into the mountains.[1] He gathers various plants from various locations in the mountains and tastes each one. A smile comes across his face. The show cuts to him in the kitchen of his restaurant, where he is now seen crafting a dish using the ingredients he discovered in the mountains. Classical music plays in the background as he uses tweezers to arrange different colors and textures and tastes into a magnificent work of beauty on a clean, white plate.

He does this same trick several more times, taking these beautiful ingredients and arranging them into something even more beautiful. Thanks to the modern miracle of high-definition technology, the images on the screen look almost edible, like I could go over to my TV and lick the screen and be transported to some flavorful fantasy of taste and texture.

Instead I make myself a plate of macaroni and hot dogs and applesauce, just like the plates I made for my three kids. I'd be lying if I said I wasn't a bit disappointed with the reality that was in front of me.

And then it hits me.

This is exactly what I feel like when I try to pray.

Jesus makes some audacious claims about prayer. He says that whatever we ask for, we can have, if we would only believe. He says that if we trust him, we can look at mountains and see them moved into the sea. He says that if we keep banging on his door, we will eventually get what we're asking for. He says that God is our loving Heavenly Father, who wants to give us good things. And he won't trick us. If we ask for bread, he's not going to give us stones. If we ask for fish, he's not going to give us snakes.

And then Paul, one of Jesus' most devout followers, tells us that, somehow, there exists an experience in prayer that is so transcendent, so moving, that it feels like heaven. Or more literally, like a "third heaven." Which is to say that it is the highest feeling of connection and nearness we humans can have with the Divine.

John, another one of Jesus' most devout followers, tells us something along these same lines. Exiled onto the island of Patmos for his beliefs, John finds himself caught up in an experience of prayer so deeply moving that it literally transforms the way he sees the entirety of earthly existence—the past, the present, and the future.

The list could go on. Peter finds God through prayer and lets go of his racism and bigotry. Isaiah meets God through prayer and feels something like fire on his lips and in his heart. Jonah cries out to God and, through prayer, changes his mind about his enemies and goes to serve them. David, after just having lost his son to death, goes to God through prayer and finds the strength and hope to carry on. Hannah, childless for years and full of shame, asks God for relief from her barren condition and she hears God speak to her about a coming son. Then, she finds herself pregnant and miraculously gives birth to a baby boy, just like God had said.

Perhaps one of the most moving accounts of prayer occurs when Moses hikes up a mountain and, presumably, starts to complain to God about feeling abandoned and helpless in the face of his leadership challenges. God responds by speaking to him directly, hiding him in a rock, and "passing by" him. We don't know what exactly happened in this experience, but we do know that it was powerful. So powerful that it changed Moses' face and made it glow.

And it's not just people "back then" who had these types of experiences in prayer. Jonathan Edwards, one of America's most famous and influential theologians, wrote about these same kinds of experiences often. Martin Luther, one of Protestant Christianity's most famous figures, wrote about the same thing. Catholics often get a bad rap for their highly structured and sometimes unintelligible approach to faith, but the truth is, there is a deep and rich history of Catholic men and women who have experienced the same kinds of moving encounters with God through prayer.

One of my favorite stories of a powerful prayer experience comes from Dwight Moody. Moody was a pastor and evangelist in Chicago during the late 1800s, among other things. In 1871, the great Chicago fire destroyed his church building. Discouraged and unsettled, he went to New York City with hopes to raise some money so he could rebuild his church. While there, he frequently walked the city streets, asking God to help him. On one particular walk, Moody found something greater than financial support. He famously recalled this exceptional walk:

> One day, in the city of New York—oh, what a day!—I cannot describe it, I seldom refer to it; it is almost too sacred an experience to name.... I can only say that God revealed himself to me, and I had such an experience of his love that I had to ask him to stay his hand. I went to preaching again. The sermons were not different; I did not present any new truths, and yet hundreds were converted. I would not now be placed back where I was before that blessed experience if you should give me all the world—it would be small dust in the balance.[2]

Think about what he is actually saying here. Moody had such a powerful experience of God's love through prayer that he had to ask God to *stop this experience*, because it was just too much. Like trying to drink an ocean through a straw, he says he can't take it all in. After this experience, Moody no longer wants what he used to want. He no longer sees the world the way he used to see it. The only thing that matters to him now is God and his love. Everything else is "small dust in the balance."

As a Christian, I read about these kinds of experiences and I can't help but feel a little slighted. A little inferior. And by a little, I mean a lot. On my best days, I have caught glimpses of this type of thing. I have felt God's warmth in my heart. I have sensed his nearness. I have become aware that someone else is in the room with me. But I have never, even remotely, felt like I could move a mountain. I have never rested in an assurance that anything—*anything!*—I asked for would be granted. I have never emerged from a time of prayer with a glowing face. I have never felt like I was in heaven, let alone a third heaven. I have never felt God's presence to the point of asking him to stop giving it to me.

I'm not saying any of this out of self-pity or despair. I'm not done with my life yet, and perhaps God is going to give me this type of experience down the road. But I am saying that every time I pray, I enter into that space with an awareness—a belief—that an experience like this is, at the very least, *possible*.

Alongside small seeds of faith in God's ability to give me this kind of deep experience also grow seeds of disappointment. On the scales of my prayer life, the two sides aren't even close to balancing. On one side, I have a handful of times where I have sensed God in clear, almost tangible ways. On the other side, I have a massive amount of times—uncountable—where I have sensed and felt nothing. And tucked inside this massive pile are several really dark times when prayer actually seemed to hurt my belief in God more than help it. When I knelt down to pray, poured out my heart to God, and experienced such a deafening silence, such a dark loneliness, I rose back up and I felt more resolved to *abandon* this God whom I had just prayed to.

These two things are present with me every time I pray. On the one hand, I am aware that deep, soul-transforming things are possible in prayer. On the other hand, I am aware that I do not experience them with any regularity.

And yet, here I am, unbalanced scales and all, still praying. After all these years.

I am not an overly disciplined man. Why would I eat only one donut when I could eat *three?* So I can't attribute my perseverance in prayer to rigorous self-effort or strength of will. And I also can't attribute my perseverance in prayer to a frequency of ecstatic experiences. So what is it then? Why do I keep praying in the face of near-constant disappointment?

All I can find for an explanation is what I experienced the other night when I was making dinner for my kids. My reality was macaroni and cheese and hot dogs and applesauce. But just outside of my reality, in another room off to the side of my daily responsibilities and best efforts to meet those responsibilities, was something far greater. Out of the corner of my eye, I could see a chef working on his craft. There were flowers and mountains and streams and fresh ingredients that came together to create beautiful dishes that looked like they belonged in an art museum.

I could see what was possible. I could see a different reality from my own. In the midst of my daily life, I got a glimpse of something that stretches beyond the daily grind and into eternity. I got a glimpse of a God who is over all, in all, and meets me through all.

In some ways, I'm no different from the gambling addict. I lose more than I win, so to speak. But the few wins that I do have are enough to keep me playing. To sacrifice everything else, I have to chase that feeling of winning again.

This is why I keep praying in the face of disappointment, in the face of unanswered prayers. I keep praying because, somehow, I know in my heart that there is more than what is in front of me. I know that there is a spiritual reality and God occupies it. More than that, this God is good and wise and loving and powerful and—this is really important to remember—is so far above and beyond me in his goodness and wisdom and love and power that I am not able to understand his ways.

Just like the talented chef I watch through a screen, God is able to do things that I can't even imagine. I look at leaves and roots and flowers and I see exactly that: leaves and roots and flowers. But a skilled chef looks at these same things and sees something more than what they are. He sees what they could be when prepared and arranged together. He sees the beauty they could become.

I see cancer kill.

I see savings shrink.

I see marriages end.

I see infertility go on.

I see kids struggle.

I see parts of the world getting worse instead of better.

I see parts of my heart getting worse instead of better.

I pray about these kinds of things, and a lot of others. Often. And nothing changes. At least, not yet. But instead of giving up on the whole business of prayer altogether, I keep at it. I keep praying. I keep feeling disappointed. And I keep bringing my disappointment with me into my attempts at prayer like a sidecar on a motorcycle. Because I know that my perspective on reality is limited. And there is a greater reality out there beyond whatever is currently in front of me.

What feels like God not answering me, what feels like God ignoring me and even forgetting about me, are real feelings. But I have to confront these feelings (or is it letting God confront them in me?) with the reminder that, while I am only capable of making boxed macaroni and cheese, he is capable of gathering the freshest of ingredients, the most beautiful produce and cuts of meat, and assembling them into a masterpiece of a meal. While I see only the reality that is in front of me, there is something different, something greater beyond what I can see.

The natural question that first comes up from this kind of thinking is this: *how do I know that this kind of reality exists?*

And then second: *how do I know that a God like this occupies this reality?*

The short answer is, I don't.

I don't *know* that a better, spiritual reality occupied by a loving and gracious God exists in the same way that I know that this keyboard on which I'm typing exists, this coffee I'm drinking exists, this music I'm listening to exists.

If I wanted to be a bit clever here, I could ask: How do I know that *anything* exists? How do I know that I'm not just a part of an elaborate dream in an autistic boy's mind, like the TV series *St. Elsewhere*?

I am not a philosopher and I am not under the influence of any mind-altering substances, so I might not be qualified to answer this kind of question. But I have found some help in an old Italian monk named Anselm. If you want to make it official, you can call him Saint Anselm of Canterbury. Anselm lived around the turn of the first millennium and, in certain circles, is famous for his contributions to Christian thought and practice. One of these contributions stands above the rest—at least, for me.

Anselm argued that we aren't foolish to put our faith in a spiritual reality, and even in a God who occupies this reality, because there is something in our hearts—"even a fool's heart," he says—that knows there is, indeed, *something* out there.[3] Where did this belief come from? Where did this concept that there is anything beyond our world come from? Then, to take it a step further, where did the desire to be in relationship with *something personal* come from? Where did *that* concept come from?

For Anselm, these desires for a spiritual reality occupied by a personal, spiritual being are worth paying attention to. They give us clues about the nature of reality as a whole. He concludes that the very presence of these desires is, in fact, proof that the real things exist.

C. S. Lewis says basically the same thing when he writes,

The Christian says, "Creatures are not born with desires unless satisfaction for those desires exists. A baby feels hunger: well, there is such a thing as food. A duckling wants to swim: well, there is such a thing as water. Men feel sexual desire: well, there is such a thing as sex. If I find in myself a desire which no experience in this world can satisfy, the most probable explanation is that I was made for another world. If none of my earthly pleasures satisfy it, that does not prove that the universe is a fraud. Probably earthly pleasures were never meant to satisfy it, but only to arouse it, to suggest the real thing...I must keep alive in myself the desire for my true country, which I shall not find till after death."[4]

And that's the key to praying with—and through—disappointment. Even lots of disappointment. The very presence of a desire for something better than disappointment—the very presence of a desire to see mountains moved—is an indicator that I am not yet experiencing reality in its fullest scope. As Lewis says, I am not yet in "my true country."

So I press on.

And there is good reason to believe that this simple act of pressing on does something in me. There is something about trying to follow God—the Christian word here is *obey*—even when I don't feel like it, that teaches me its own lesson, perhaps more needed than if I had an immediate entrance into a deep, holy experience. It teaches me resilience—the cowboy word here is *grit*—to follow something despite a void in my feelings, which, if nothing else, is a process that will grow my character and teach me to delay my gratification.

Lewis helps me here, again. In one of his books, he writes from the satirical perspective of a "senior devil" named Screwtape instructing a "junior devil" named Wormwood on how to tempt an unnamed man away from following the "Enemy," that is to say God. I found this thought for the first time in college and it has helped me ever since:

> Do not be deceived, Wormwood. Our cause is never more in danger than when a human, no longer desiring, but still intending, to do our Enemy's will, looks round upon a universe from which every trace of Him seems to have vanished, and asks why he has been forsaken, and still obeys.[5]

Sometimes I feel like God has vanished. I feel forsaken. I feel like I'm stuck with something less than what I want, even than what I *deserve*. I am tempted to abandon prayer and wallow in my self-pity or shake my fist toward God in my self-reliance.

Both of these happen, to be sure. Often. But when the dust settles, I still strangely find myself obeying. On my best days, I'm obeying God himself. On other, less spectacular days, though, I'm obeying an inner desire that I can't ignore, even in the face of my many disappointments. I'm obeying this belief that I can't ever seem to permanently shake off—that prayer, in all of its complexity, is something I *need*.

WHEN I FIRST became a Christian, I felt lost and found at the same time. I knew that I had found this intense, and sometimes unexplainable, interest in Jesus. And for the first time in my life, I felt like I had a true home—a home that would always welcome me, always love me, always be there for me. But I also felt a bit lost, too. Now that I had surrendered my heart and life to Jesus, what was supposed to happen next?

I looked to other Christians for help. Older, wiser men and women of the faith graciously answered my questions, endured my doubts, and gently guided me toward a life of faith. One of my favorite lines in any poem comes from Alfred, Lord Tennyson's "Ulysses," where he writes, "I am a part of all that I have met." As I write these words now, I see just how true this is. Without the patient support of the Christian community—both then and now—I wouldn't be the person I am today. I'm grateful.

Looking back on my early years of faith, I remember a few specific things that fellow travelers told me to do. One of these was called a "quiet time." For the Christians that I was around, this was considered the bedrock of Christian practice. And it goes like this: God has given us this great gift of the Bible. It's through this ancient text that he most often and most clearly speaks to people. So if you want to grow in your relationship with him, you need to read the Bible. As much as possible. Now you also have to live your normal life, too. It probably isn't realistic for someone to read the Bible every day, all day, but you need to do *something*. And that something looked like getting up early in the morning before you started your day, opening up the Bible in a quiet place, and reading.

I don't remember anyone telling me how long I was supposed to read, but I gathered through various conversations that five minutes was too short and even an hour might not be long enough.

Oh—and the most important part was I had to be *quiet*. Hence the name.

These same well-meaning people also told me I had to do other things like go to church as often as possible, throw away all of my music that wasn't "Christian" (I wasn't always sure what that meant), and if I was really serious about growing in my faith, limit my friendships with people who drank or smoked or slept with people that they weren't married to. This was hard for me to understand because that meant I had to stop hanging out with virtually all of my non-Christian friends. While they were keen on the sleeping-with-someone part, they weren't too keen on the getting-married-while-still-in-high-school part.

When it came to money, they taught me that being generous is one of the most important ways we can connect with

God. So it would be a good idea to start giving away part of my paycheck, too. Along these same lines, I was told that if I was really serious about growing with God, I should also go to another country—or at least some inner city in America with poor people in it—on a mission trip.

And here's the thing about all of this—I *wanted* to do these things. For me, Jesus was everything. And if completely overhauling my life and reorganizing it around these practices would lead to deeper experiences with him, I was all in. I was willing to do whatever it took to grow.

I remember one of my Christian friends was the son of a pastor. He led a Bible study at our high school, which is funny when you think about it because we weren't old enough to buy cigarettes, but there he was, explaining the Trinity with confidence. The benefit of youth is that you don't know what you don't know, which only makes you more sure of what you do know. It's like growing up in New Hampshire and thinking you know about mountains. Eventually you go to Colorado and then you see *mountains* and you realize that you were naïve. And then you replay all of your pontificating about mountains to other people and you want to find a phone and call all of them to say, "Remember that time I was telling you about mountains. Well, I've been to a different place where they have *real mountains* and you're never going to believe this…"

It's a miracle that any of us still believe today. The blind leading the blind doesn't begin to cover it. God is, if anything, merciful.

One of the things I remember about this friend is that he had a Bible that was huge. If our little Bible study was the NBA, he had the Dikembe Mutombo of Bibles. And it was sturdy like a butcher's block. It was navy blue with silver gilded pages and two ribbons for marking where you were reading. It even had his name imprinted on the cover in a font that looked like something from *The Lord of the Rings*. It was beautiful.

Until it wasn't. After about a year or so, this Bible looked ragged and worn. Like someone had tied it to the back of a truck and dragged it through a desert. The faux leather was cracked. The ribbons were frayed. The silver on the edge of the pages was wearing off. It looked almost abused.

I asked my friend why he let such a beautiful book fall into such disrepair. He looked at me and explained, "Well, I read this thing all the time. Used things should look used."

I sheepishly slid my glossy, unused-looking Bible behind my back and nodded.

I also remember hearing about something called a "prayer list." Initially I wasn't sure what this was, but I eventually learned that Christians were supposed to ask people if they could pray for them. This included relatives, friends, the waiter at the restaurant, the woman cleaning your teeth at the dentist's office—anyone, really. When someone would respond with a request—"Could you pray for my brother? He isn't working right now and can't find a job."—you now had a decision to make. I was never sure of the criteria for how this got decided, but somehow you had two responses to these requests. You could say something like, "Sure, I'll pray for you about that." Or for unknown reasons that I still haven't figured out, you might take your commitment to pray for this request one step further and say, "I'll add you to my prayer list."

As I was trying to figure out the social norms of my new Christian circles of influence, this particular practice was anxiety-inducing. From a very early age, I have always lived with a high awareness of things. Some personality tests call this "conscientiousness," which means that I notice it when one of my shoelaces is pulled longer on one side of my shoes and it bothers me until I can unlace the entire thing, pull the two sides of the lace to the same length on each side, and then re-lace the shoe.

And it gets worse. Not only do I notice things like this, but also I feel *responsible* for them. Over-responsible, actually. If I see something that needs fixing, or could at least be made better, I feel an underlying sense of duty to fix it, to make it better.

Now imagine this idea of a prayer list entering into my young faith. I wanted to be a good, strong Christian. In my mind, part of becoming a good, strong Christian meant that I had to pray for other people. More than that, I wanted to. So I asked the people within my life if I could pray for them. They responded by giving me things to pray for. I then had to decide which bucket I was going to put that request in. Do I put it in the "I'll pray about that" bucket, or do I put it in the "prayer list" bucket? And how do you know which bucket it belongs in? Aren't all requests meaningful to God? Don't they all deserve my attention? Who am I to say that my friend's request for prayer about his overdramatic girlfriend isn't as important as my other friend's request for his dad to stop drinking? Which one gets a spot on my prayer list?

And that's only the half of it. Because once I made the decision to add a request to my prayer list, I felt the responsibility to pray about it. Which introduced another layer of questions, and anxiety.

How long do I have to pray for this request?
Until it's answered?
Or until I feel "released" from praying for it?
And what about all these other requests I feel responsible for?
Some of them are years old.
And I don't even like some of these people anymore.
Do I still have to pray for them?
Or can I remove them from the list?

This was a big deal for me. I truly wanted to do what I was supposed to do, to do what would grow me into the man that Jesus wanted me to be. I didn't want to let anyone down. And I didn't want to cheat anyone out of a prayer that they might have desperately needed. But sometimes I felt like I was in an imaginary conversation with God. It went like this:

God: Adam, I would have loved to intervene in your friend's troubles at school. But you and your cold heart crossed him off your prayer list the day before I was going to answer those prayers for him because you said you "had too much to pray for already." So instead I just let those troubles continue.

Me: Wait...what?

God: Yeah. You know how your friend told you that he was feeling lonely because he didn't have any friends at school? I was just about to give a girl's dad in Maryland a promotion that would have brought her and her family to your friend's neighborhood. They would have met in a few weeks, fallen in love, and eventually gotten married after college. But not anymore.

Me: Well, that sucks.

God: I know, right?

Me: I'm really sorry.

God: I know. The real kicker is their future daughter was going to be the one to cure cancer, too.

Me: You're kidding.

God: Nope.

Me: You're not going to tell my friend that it's my fault he's still lonely and that he doesn't get to marry this great girl and one day have a daughter that cures cancer, are you?

[*long pause*]

God: I haven't decided yet.

Regardless of our varied experiences and backgrounds, denominations, and faith traditions, Christians throughout history have agreed that praying for other people is essential to our relationship with God and his world. If this is true, and I believe that it is, how do we pray for others in a way that brings meaning and life to our hearts without overwhelming us?

I think the way forward looks more like empathy than responsibility. Yes—both Jesus and Paul tell us that, if we are Christians, we are responsible for looking after each other. An eye can't tell the hand it isn't important, a hand can't tell a foot that it doesn't matter, etc. Like all of God's moral commands, they are given to us not so that we can focus on our responsibility within them. Not forever, at least. For example, when we first hear that we are supposed to give time, money, and resources to the poor, the only motivation that might break through our selfish, self-centered hearts is that of responsibility. We initially change our spending habits and give to the poor because we feel responsible for obeying the God we say we love—and who certainly loves us. And we might even feel a bit responsible for the person or group of people we seek to help.

But we all know that this sense of responsibility will be short-lived if something greater than a sense of responsibility doesn't come in and take its place. Eventually we will want to buy a new car or to take a vacation or to save more for retirement, and whatever sense of responsibility we used to feel will cave to a fresh sense of reason or a pressing sense of responsibility to our latest circumstances, which might even just be a cloaked sense of responsibility in our own selves.

Take, as another example, a wedding. A bride and a groom stand before each other, friends, and family, and commit their lives and love to each other through various forms of beauty and ceremony. Someone might read a passage from the Bible. Another might sing a song or read a poem or share a funny story. Hopefully the pastor doesn't preach too long—or at all, for that matter. Weddings aren't for preaching, but for encouragement and celebration and prayer and *kissing*. Most likely the bride and groom will exchange rings. And they will most likely exchange something called vows, too.

Make no mistake: This vows part is what really matters. When the bride and groom share their vows, whether traditional in nature or self-written or downloaded from Google, they are saying to each other that they are knowingly (as much as is possible, at least) entering into an agreement with each other. And this agreement is designed to give our hearts what they most want in a relationship—assurance. To know that another person will stay with you, no matter what, should lead to great peace, and even contentment. Very often a marriage doesn't feel like this, but that's the idea behind the vows. Ideally, they remind us that we won't be left alone. Which is why they are so beautiful.

Whenever I see two people say these kinds of things to each other, I can't help but feel a lump start to grow in my throat, which then shimmies up my face and tries to make its way out of my eye ducts in the form of tears. I always end up playing it cool and swallowing hard so I can avoid an ugly cry. But I am moved. I am moved because of the nature of what's happening in these vows.

It's easy to see something like vows solely from the sense of responsibility. Meaning, in this wedding example, that the bride and the groom make these grand pronouncements of a future love that they have no real idea about. They have no idea if they will be able to endure their spouse's firing from a workplace, their spouse's sickness, their spouse's depression, their spouse's affair. They have no idea if they will be able to still love and be loved in the face of infertility, addiction, the death of one of their parents, God forbid the death of one of their children. They simply don't. No one standing in that place does. But the initial hope in these vows is that, when the feelings of love fade, when one of the partners in a marriage agreement feels like giving up, he or she will wake up every morning, take a long look in the mirror, and under the sense of responsibility to these vows that were said long ago, stay in the fight. That he or she will stay faithful to their partner even if feelings are no longer there, even if that spouse feels like an enemy. That they will keep loving the other person even if they don't want to keep loving because they are responsible to their spouse, to their own previous promises, to God.

Of course, sometimes this is how it truly is in marriage. A sense of responsibility might be the only thing that keeps someone staying in the relationship. And well and good that there is that sense of responsibility. That might be enough to sustain someone through a season of recklessness, self-pity, resentment, hurt, or whatever else is trying to pry his or her heart away from his or her spouse.

But most of us have personally known marriages in which this sense of responsibility either ran out or became the only reason why a husband or a wife remained in the relationship. In both cases, brokenness ensued.

Responsibility isn't enough to make a marriage really flourish, just as it isn't enough to make our relationship with God—including our prayer lives—flourish. We need something more than duty to sustain us.

Now, how does all of this relate to how we can be better at praying for others?

I was watching a documentary about design the other day and I heard a profound statement.[1] Partly I think it was so profound because the woman saying it was British and anything I hear spoken with a British accent sounds profound to me. In any case, the woman was an interior designer named Ilse Crawford, whom I knew nothing about. She was talking about how she starts her process for a new project. Sandwiched in between some specifics she went through about main ideas and textures and clients, she said something so quick that I almost missed it the first time and had to go back and hear it again to make sure that she wasn't just giving me some drivel that I assumed was profound because it sounded like a queen saying it.

She said that *empathy* is the foundation of design.

This was not what I'd expected to hear in the slightest.

But as soon as I heard those words, I felt them ricochet in my heart, and I knew they were true.

The documentary went on to show Mrs. Crawford—I'm going to call her "Mrs." because she is married and British, which commands some respect in my book—trying out several chairs. She compared their height, their width, the pitch of their seats, the texture of their materials, their colors, their lines. Then she walked over to a big white wall where she had hung dozens and dozens of Post-it Notes. On these colored squares she had written individual words or thoughts that defined the environment she was designing for. She pulled back from the wall of notes, thought for a minute, and then said something that drew her back into her project, talking about luxury or warmth or feelings of connection and community.

Because of her profession, and I can only assume because of the contract she negotiated, which I can also only assume included an exchange of a large sum of money, Mrs. Crawford had a responsibility to perform her duties well. What fascinated me, though, was seeing her move past *responsibility* and into *empathy*—a real awareness not of what *she* felt or desired, but instead an awareness of what *her client* felt and desired. And then, even more so, what *the intended users* of her client's space felt and would feel, desired and would desire while they were using the space that she was tasked to create.

It was amazing to watch.

All of this has implications for how we pray for others. M. Scott Peck, who wasn't British but still said a lot of profound things, wrote three of the most famous and truthful words ever recorded. He simply said, "Life is difficult."[2] Donald Miller, a more contemporary author, said it this way: "It's a hard thing to be a human. It's a very hard thing."[3] Both have it right. Life is difficult. And to be a human being in the midst of this difficulty adds its own set of hardships, mainly the issue of having a conscious thing inside you called a soul that feels disappointment and pain and longing and emptiness and fear.

Peter Kreeft, a Catholic writer who also is a philosophy professor, humanizes this experience of difficulty for us when he writes:

> Your neighbor, your best friend, your doctor, your auto mechanic all have deep and hidden hurts that you don't know about, just as you have some that they don't know about. Everybody out there is hurting. And if you don't know that, you're either very naïve and believe in people's facades, or so thick-skinned that you don't hurt yourself and don't feel other people's hurts either.[4]

And here we have it. Mrs. Crawford and Peter Kreeft are saying the same thing, albeit in different ways. For the designer, life is full of problems to be solved. The chair is too tall. The table is too short. The space is too cluttered. The hallway is too plain. If the designer wants to solve these problems in ways that add beauty and value to the lives of those involved, she must first practice *empathy*—she must first get into the skin, so to speak, of what it's like for the people experiencing the problem. The more empathy she can find, the greater her insights will be.

For the person who prays for someone else, we have the same job. Everyone we pray for carries with them a certain measure of pain, whether from their past or from their present realities of life. We certainly can pray without empathy, but sooner or later, our prayers will take on an unnecessary seriousness about them. And most of us only can stand so much seriousness before we grow bored or tired of it, and then we shirk it off. We might like a sense of responsibility, but not for too long. Duty isn't enough to sustain us. We need something more.

More than we are responsible for praying for others, we are called to have empathy for them. Which should, then, lead us to pray for them. Not because we feel a sense of duty, but instead because we feel a sense of community with them. Life is hard. *My* life is hard. *Your* life is hard. Maybe not in the same ways or to the same degree, but we both experience whatever hardships we face as human beings. We *all* breathe. We *all* bleed. These commonalities should lead us toward a greater understanding of how much we need to be understood, and to give the gift of understanding to someone else who shares that same need. And then to give them our prayers born out of this understanding.

Sometimes examples help us, so let me provide a quick one to help flesh this out a bit. Somehow you discover that one of your friends has just gotten the news that he has cancer. The doctors are still running tests and determining what stage the cancer is in, but it doesn't look good. Your friend is married and has kids that are just about to go to college. You're not sure about his relationship with God, but you have had a few spiritual conversations with him in the past several years. You know that his marriage hasn't been great. You also know that he feels a lot of pressure from work.

As you find out this sobering news, you feel like you should commit to pray for him. That's an initial sense of responsibility working in you, which is good. It moves you to act. So maybe you pray something like this:

God, please be with Michael. He's got cancer. Please heal him. Please be with his family. Amen.

This is how most of us would pray in a situation like this. I don't think it's a bad prayer—who am I to criticize anyone's prayers? I think God likes it whenever any of his kids talk to him. But I do think this prayer could go deeper. And empathy is the key.

What if you tried this little exercise before you prayed for the people in your life who are hurting? What if you tried, as best as you can, to put yourself in their shoes? To temporarily feel what they feel, to face what they face? What if you tried to move past a sense of responsibility—of *should*—and into a real sense of empathy for the people you're praying for?

Back to your friend Michael. Maybe before you pray for

him (or anyone that you are praying for, really), you pause for a moment. Before you *speak* to God about him, you *ask* God about him.

God, what's it like for Michael to hear the news that he might not live to walk his daughter down the aisle when she gets married?

What's it like for him to have to keep working, keep meeting deadlines, while at the same time he's trying to go to doctor's appointments and call insurance representatives and prepare his soul for what might be coming?

What's it like for him to think about death and what comes afterward without having a sure faith in someone like you?

I bet he feels scared.

I bet he feels alone.

I bet he feels angry.

If we can slow down and put ourselves in someone else's position—even if it's just for a few minutes—we get a better picture of how we can pray for them. We still remain on the outside of their specific suffering. But asking these kinds of questions, and then doing our best to really think about how we would feel if we were in someone else's position, helps us move past the rote exercise of a prayer list and into something alive in our prayers. Beyond a high view of God and his character, empathy for others is the greatest gift we can experience in our prayer lives. If we can somehow experience empathy for those we pray for, it will change the way that we pray:

God, Michael is facing a horrible situation. I can't imagine what he is feeling. But I'm sure he's scared about the future. It's all so unknown right now and I'm sure he feels out of control. He might be angry at you, God. And he might feel deeply alone. God, please be near to Michael right now. Give him peace about the future and let him know that you are in control. Let him know that you will be with him through whatever he faces. Also let him know that it's okay to be angry and the best place for his anger isn't in his relationship with his wife or his kids or his coworkers, but it's with you. I pray that he can be honest with you about how mad he is, how unfair he thinks this is, how scared he is. I pray that you send people into his life that can help him with his loneliness—if there's anything specific I can do, speak to me about that, God. I pray that you help the doctors and nurses to have compassion for Michael. Give him favor with his insurance company. Give him moments of intimacy with his wife. Give him a season of easiness at work. Most important, give him you, God. Use this diagnosis to clear the paths in his heart for your grace. Help him to trust you. Help me to trust you, as well. Amen.

This—or something like this—is what happens when we can slow down and pray with empathy. We become aware of what is really going on in the lives and hearts of those we are praying for. And it causes us to pray with a greater awareness of what is needed.

If all of this sounds time-consuming, you're right. It is. But like most things, we get better at it the more that we do it. Initially, it might feel very foreign for us to try and pray with empathy for others. This is for a lot of reasons, but they all come down to the fact that we are selfish and self-centered and that makes us clumsy when we try to get outside ourselves and think of others.

But as we keep practicing this little step, we will see our own hearts grow a little less selfish. Anytime we take steps to become less selfish, no matter how small they are, we find free-dom on the other side. It's like hiking a hard trail and then getting to the top of the ridge and finding the reward of a per-fect view.

Which is a pretty good way to think about prayer.

8 WORRY

MY PRAYER LIFE has many enemies. Some of them are even my fault. I am not a morning person (as it should be *very* clear by now, this far into the book)—my fault. I prefer the warmth and comfort of my bed over the cold, dark nothingness of 5:00 a.m.—my fault again. My mind wanders when I try to pray—not one hundred percent my fault, but enough of my fault to make me feel a little guilty about it. I get bored praying the same things over and over again, even if they are good things to pray for—probably my fault.

One of the greatest enemies of my prayer life that is, without question, my fault is how much I worry. In fact, if I could change one thing about myself, it would be to worry less. I'm not sure why I worry so much. I do have some ideas, but that almost isn't even the point. When you're shivering and achy and throwing up because you have the flu, it doesn't matter *how* you contracted it. What matters is the havoc it creates in your life. And more important, what you are going to do about it, how you are going to try to get healthy again.

Worry is a dangerous activity for our hearts. Because, at the center of any worry that we might have is a desire to be in control. When we worry that we will be late for our meeting, we worry because we can't control the traffic that is in front of us or the elevator that is taking too long or even our own laziness that caused us to sleep through five alarms. When we worry about our health, we worry because we can't control our genetics or our cholesterol levels or our addiction to tobacco or our aversion to exercise. We worry about our kids for the same reasons. We can't control whom they date, how they study, where they go when they back out of the driveway. And the same goes for our jobs. We can't control how other people perceive us, how much profit will come in, how many promotions will open up, or if our company will have to lay people off.

The list could go on. And on.

One of the few constants in our lives is this absence of control. If you think about it long enough, you will realize just how little control you actually have. In any area of your life, really. This lack of control often leads us to feelings of insecurity, fear, and vulnerability. And not in the "I'm being vulnerable by telling you about my secret desires or sins" kind of way—which is actually a bit noble—but more in the "I'm in the woods alone and I see a big bear running at me with anger in his eyes and I feel vulnerable to death right now because I don't have a gun or even some of that special spray made for bears so I'm definitely about to die for sure" kind of way.

And the bear keeps coming.

We want to be in control of our lives. Maybe not in *total* control, but control nonetheless. We want to be able to determine how long we will live, how much money we will make, how we will be loved, how our kids will turn out, even how the weather will be on our vacation. You may not feel like you want to control these things, but pause for a minute and examine what happens to your heart when these things—or *anything*, really—don't go your way. Chances are you feel frustrated. You might feel a lot of other things, too, but this underlying feeling of frustration is an indicator of something your soul is trying to tell you. It wants happiness. Probably more than anything else. And the way that most of us define happiness is an absence of frustration. Or to put it another way, happiness is a security brought about by our ability to be in control of our own lives. And, quite often, of other people's lives, too.

I wish that I could say that all of this is my idea—the result of long hours in prayer and meditation and countless journeys of the heart in which I climbed the very mountain of God and met him face-to-face, returning back to earth with a shining face of my own and a glorious heart. But it's far less spectacular than this. Beyond my own experience, I know this from the earliest story in the Bible.

Earlier I wrote about Adam and Eve and how they ate the fruit from the only tree in their garden that God said not to. I wrote about how the serpent tempted Adam and Eve toward pride, which showed itself primarily through ingratitude, and how dangerous it is for our souls to continue in prayer without gratitude as one of our chief guides.

But there was something else going on in this ancient story, as well. Beyond Adam and Eve's initial fall from the perfect, grace-filled state of the garden, they *continued* to fall—in almost ridiculous, even absurd fashion. The story tells us that once Adam and Eve disobeyed God and rebelled against his leadership and authority in their lives, they immediately started to see things differently. Well, actually they started to see *everything* differently. The coaxing serpent became an enemy. Their nakedness became an embarrassment. The garden became a hiding place. And their Father became a Judge.

The story doesn't tell us this explicitly, but I think it's more than fair to say that Adam and Eve felt a tremendous amount of worry. The first two chapters of this story move at an almost leisurely pace, like a canoe drifting lazily down a winding river. But once Adam and Eve break their covenant with God, the narrative picks up into a panic. The slow, easy life they had previously experienced with God is now a life frantic with hiding. And problem-solving.

Once they realize their own nakedness, and consequently feel shame, Adam and Eve—for the first time in their lives—try to *fix* something. Before their sin, God was the one who created everything. Because God is good and perfect, nothing needed to be fixed. Nothing needed to be solved. But now that sin had entered into Creation, there were problems. Mainly, this issue of having no clothes. So Adam and Eve set about solving this problem and they came up with this solution: they would take an animal's life, remove its skin, make some coverings out of this skin, and put them on as clothes.

The order here is important. First, Adam and Eve felt insecure. They wondered if there was something better than what they were experiencing. And instead of trusting in God's control, they decided to take control of their own lives. They ate the forbidden fruit—they took something that didn't belong to them, that they were not given. This went badly. In order to deal with the harmful consequences of their decision, Adam and Eve again took something that did not belong to them, that they were not given—an animal's life. Then, they took the skin from this animal and wore it as clothing. Problem solved. No more dealing with this embarrassing thing called "nakedness."

Do you see what's going on here?

Pride and ingratitude were there from the beginning. But so was something else: *worry*. Adam and Eve worried that they weren't experiencing the things that they should be experiencing. And in response to this feeling of worry, they tried to exercise control in a situation that they were never designed to control. All of this only resulted in more worry—*Why are we naked? We shouldn't be naked. We need to solve this problem of nakedness.* And control—*Let's kill that cow over there and use its skin for our second layer of skin that will hide our skin. Let's call this second skin "clothes."*

This is another one of our problems as human beings. When we're not in control, or even when we come up against the limits of control, we can't help but feel insecure and afraid and small and start to worry. We end up spending our emotional, physical, and spiritual energy on this feeling of worry, which is to say that we use whatever faculties we have available at the time to try to control things that we can't. Like the hamster on the spinning wheel, we make a lot of effort that ultimately gets us nowhere.

Drilling down a bit deeper, think about the problems you're most concerned with right now. Maybe it's your health. Maybe it's your job. Maybe it's your children. Almost certainly it's your future. In all of these, you want to be able to control what happens to you. And there may be aspects of your past that still bother you—you wish you could go back and control those, too. The cold, hard reality that we all must face is that we can't control any of this. We can't make our genes behave the way we want them to. We can't make our jobs give us the security we want them to. We can't make our kids turn out the way we want them to. We can't control our future—there are simply too many factors in play. And we certainly can't control our past—what happened has happened.

And yet the majority of us spend an incredible amount of time trying to control all of these things. We can't make any serious headway into any of them, which leaves us feeling frustrated. And there are only two responses to frustration: give up or fight harder. Picture a man lying underneath a bench press bar. On both sides of the bar are stacks and stacks of weights— more than he has ever lifted before. Optimistically he reaches up, wraps his hands around the bar, gives it a slight lift so it comes out of its cradle, and then slowly lowers it onto his chest. When he tries to reverse the motion and raise the bar back up, he stalls. The bar is H-E-A-V-Y. So heavy, in fact, that he's not sure if he can lift it up to put it back in the cradle. In an instant, he goes from relative ease to frustration. He wants something that isn't coming easily. In this same instant, he probably worries. He wants control. He has a choice to make: either give up and ask his lifting partner for help or fight harder to push the bar back up.

Here is where all of this starts to speak to the way that we pray. Every one of us will, inevitably, face things in our lives that don't go the way we want them to. We will most likely worry about them. We will feel frustrated by them, mainly because we can't control them. We will also end up making one of these two choices: we will either give up or we will try harder to exert our control over the situation.

What makes worry so dangerous to our attempts at prayer is that God tells us to do neither of these things. When we face things that we can't control and we find our hearts in a state of frustration, he doesn't want us to give up. And he doesn't want us to simply try harder, either.

Jesus talked a lot about prayer, but one of my favorite stories he gives us has to do with a woman who lost her husband. (See Luke 18:1–8.) Apparently she lost him through some type of injustice because, in an attempt to deal with her pain and loss, she went to find a judge. She hoped that he would right whatever wrongs she had suffered. At first, the judge ignored her. While this might seem cruel to us, it actually wasn't that unusual in this historical setting. During that time period, women did not possess the same rights as men. This affected many areas of society, including the legal process. A woman asking for justice—sadly—didn't mean very much. Especially if her adversaries were men. So while the judge might have been acting cruelly, he was more than likely just treating this woman like he would have treated all women—as not worthy of his time. Thank God that he doesn't treat us this way, and that's most certainly not the point of Jesus' story. What should stand out to us is what happens next.

Jesus tells us that the woman remained persistent. Even though she was being ignored, she kept knocking at this judge's door. She didn't give up. Even when she was experiencing frustration, and we can only assume worry as well, she stayed after the judge to the point of "bothering" him. Jesus, with no doubt a sense of humor, tells us that the judge finally answered her request simply because he didn't want to be "beat down" by her any longer.

We shouldn't pass over all of this too quickly. In this story, we have a woman who suffered under things she couldn't control—losing her husband. She now finds herself in a state of continued suffering and, again, facing things she can't control—dealing with a reticent judge. Most people would give up after a few days of knocking. But she doesn't. She keeps knocking at this judge's door. And then he eventually opens up and gives her what she wants.

Jesus couldn't be clearer here. In the face of frustration and worry, we are not to give up. He wants us to keep going to the God who can help us. If this widow had retreated to her own frustration and worry, perhaps she would have become depressed or bitter or resentful or, even worse, *evil*. Perhaps she would have spent the next few years plotting revenge on this judge and then one day taken all of the anger of losing her husband and then being denied justice out on this judge in an evil act of murder. But by not giving up, she kept her heart warm to what she really needed: someone from the outside, who possessed more power than what she possessed, to intervene.

When we face frustration, giving up on God is certainly an option, but not a good one. Which means that worry isn't really a good option, either, because worry is a form of giving up on God. When we worry, we say to God, "I can't trust you to control this situation in my life, so I'll just go ahead and take control of it myself." Within a single act of worry, we surrender our trust in God in exchange for a trust in ourselves. Which is ludicrous because God is the one we really need. And for mostly mysterious reasons, he has told us time and again that there is something about our trust in him that draws him into engagement with our lives.

I think this is what Jesus wants to show us about prayer in this story. When we are frustrated and feel like things are beyond our control, he wants us to put our trust in him. He wants us to go to him instead of going to our own emotion of worry.

And sometimes the way that we put our trust in him is by beating down his door.

If giving up isn't an option when we face frustration, neither is trying harder. This might sound a bit contradictory to the story I just talked about. Didn't the widow try harder when she kept knocking? On the surface, yes, she did. But stepping back a bit, we see the broader point that Jesus was trying to make. Jesus was speaking to Jews, specifically his disciples. They would have had an understanding of God that went something like this:

God is good.

We are not.

The way that we please God is by trying harder to be better than what we are.

If we try hard enough, and become good enough, then God will be pleased with us.

Then God will do things for us, like answer our prayers.

Initially this might even sound like your understanding of God. Do a quick test to see: When something bad happens to you, do you go to a place of guilt and shame for some past sin or behavior you have done? Do you think that God is punishing you for your wrong actions or decisions by bringing whatever bad thing you're experiencing into your life? And then, consequently, do you feel a pressure to start "living right" again, often marked by a renewed commitment to reading the Bible or going to church or praying or even getting rebaptized?

I knew I had this coming. If I had just lived a little better, if I had just tried a little harder to be good, then this wouldn't have happened. God must be angry at me. He must be punishing me.

If this is how you see God, then you are just like the disciples. This type of understanding of God and how he treats us is so common that it is almost like carbon monoxide poisoning. It is odorless, tasteless, and impossible to see, but it is everywhere and it will most certainly kill you. The only way to detect it is by bringing in special tools to find it. These kinds of questions are those tools.

When we see God as a parole officer who gives us redemption only if we toe the line and obey his rules, we distort his character and we rebel against the core nature of his redemptive work. God doesn't save the people who try really hard to be good. He saves the people who know they can never be good enough, so they stop trying to save themselves altogether and instead open their hands to grace. The line can never be toed enough. So instead God paints over the line with his Son's blood.

And then he invites us in.

There are a few images that are helpful to me to see and even experience what prayer should feel like. One of them goes like this: I am in a room somewhere in a house. Sometimes I'm sitting in a chair and sometimes I'm kneeling and sometimes I'm lying down half-asleep. There's some light in the room coming from a window so I can see. At some point I take a step out of the room and I am in a hallway. As I get to the hallway, I see another room. The door is open just enough for me to see that there is a much brighter light inside it. Not only is this light brighter, but it's warmer, too. And better than the light I had in my room. Before I take a step toward this other room, I know that there is someone in there who is inviting me into his presence. So I go. As I enter into this second room, I see Jesus. His eyes are full of tenderness, and his face is warm and glowing with love. And he smiles at me.

That's one way to think about the entire Christian life, and specifically about prayer. God invites us in. And the way that we accept his invitation to come into his presence has nothing to do with our ability to try harder. It has to do with our willingness to receive his invitation.

Jesus talks about this idea when he says these powerful words that I keep coming back to in this book:

Are you tired? Worn out? Burned out on religion? Come to me. Get away with me and you'll recover your life. I'll show you how to take a real rest. Walk with me and work with me—watch how I do it. Learn the unforced rhythms of grace. I won't lay anything heavy or ill-fitting on you. Keep company with me and you'll learn to live freely and lightly. (Matthew 11:28–30 MSG)

"Come to me." "Get away with me." "Walk with me." "Work with me." "Keep company with me." These are all expressions of intimacy. An intimacy that marks a life with God that is not contingent upon our effort, but upon his mercy and grace and power to create space for us in himself.

When we feel tempted to worry about the things we can't control, or whatever is frustrating us, we have to admit that we are also feeling tempted to somehow find a work-around from God. We are the naked ones standing in a garden, trying to fix our embarrassment and shame. Instead of going directly to God and asking him for help, we try to solve our problem by appealing to our own resourcefulness. In many ways, we try harder. Meaning, we resort to our self-sufficiency. We come up with the plan to kill the animal, pull off its skin, and wear it around ourselves. And the beginning of all this is a heart that is *worried*.

How many times do we do this in our lives? Too many to count. One of our kids is struggling with school, so we make a schedule for homework and meet with her teachers and maybe even revoke the privilege of extracurricular activities—all with the hopes of improving the outlook of the situation. Our job isn't going the way that we want it to go, so we put our head down and work even harder, arriving early and staying late. We try to position ourselves in the right circles of the office politics. Maybe we even start to look for another job. We're not happy with our health or maybe even just the way that our body stares back at us in the mirror, so we restrict our diet, join a gym, throw away the cake. We try anything that will help us.

That's not to say that any of this is wrong. In fact, some of these things might actually reflect a much-needed change in lifestyle or values or behaviors. But if these renewed efforts and attempts at problem-solving spring from a sense of worry, a desire for control, or a feeling of frustration, we are doomed. Because God didn't design us this way.

Instead of *worry*, God made us to *trust* in his provision.

Instead of *control*, God made us to *yield* to his kingly power and authority.

Instead of *frustration*, God made us to *rest* in his will and ways.

These are our real enemies when we pray.

And these things are what we need when we pray. A heart that trusts in God's full provision for us instead of spinning around in its own empty worry. A heart that yields to God as a King instead of wanting to be its own king. A heart that rests in God's tender and loving hands instead of railing against his will in frustration.

Sometimes a feeling of worry is the best that we can do. Our hearts are conditioned to take responsibility in so many ways that it's hard to avoid a sense of worry when we feel like so many things are out of our control, or are frustrating. Ideally, we wouldn't worry. We would be able to face our lives with a firm conviction and strength that God is with us. And that he is the True King who will work on our behalf so we neither give up nor do we rest on our own resourcefulness when we face things that we can't control. But I realize that sometimes this is all but impossible to actually live out. Worry creeps in like an uninvited houseguest we wish would leave, but instead we discover that he has unpacked his bags and plans to stay for a week. Or a month. Maybe *years*.

It is important to remember that Jesus gives us kindness in these moments, in these seasons. As he did with Adam and Eve, he calls out to us. He comes to find us. He talks with us. And he gives us grace.

When we feel overcome with worry, we need to remember this. We need to remember that God's love is infinitely patient and wise and kind. He can extend past our worry and into our restless hearts.

And we also need to remember this, too: if we are going to worry, we need to at least make sure that we are worrying in God's direction.

Because sometimes prayer is nothing more than worrying toward God, hoping in him even in the midst of our weakness.

9 SILENCE

IF SOMEONE WERE to hand you a Bible and ask you to open it, chances are you would land somewhere in the middle. In the middle rests one of the most important books in the entire Bible. In this book you would find all that you need to know about talking with God. You would see examples of how to bring your requests to him with courage and boldness. You would see examples of how to cry out to him in desperation. You would even see examples of how to pray *against* your enemies. Even your *enemies' babies*. Specifically, their heads. Mainly, that they would be bashed against some rocks.

The Psalms are, if anything, honest.

And they are also helpful. Eugene Peterson has written a great deal about how we grow in our relationship with God. One of my favorite books he wrote has to do with the Psalms.[1] In his book *Answering God*—what a great title, full of implications: God speaks first, we answer him, he hears us, etc.—he writes about how children learn language. Peterson says that children do not learn how to speak to people through complicated grammar lessons or tedious tasks of pronunciation.

Instead, they learn how to speak by first being spoken to. In other words, they *listen*. They receive a message, which in turn trains them to know how to come up with messages of their own.

Any parent who has raised babies into children and has watched this process firsthand knows what Peterson is talking about. Even if we don't intentionally try to enact this process, we still intuitively find ourselves doing it.

I remember when our first daughter was born. My wife went into labor in the middle of the night—around midnight—and we rushed off to the hospital. After her initial check-in, we settled down and prepared to meet our new baby girl. No one told us that part of the preparation would include several long walks down the white hospital halls, all in an attempt to loosen our stubborn little lady's grip on her mom's uterus so we could finally meet her. And no one told us about something called "back labor," which apparently means that the baby's skull is positioned in such a way against her mom's backbone that anytime a contraction would come, excruciating pain would also come. Not for the baby. And not for the dad, either. This special gift of grace was reserved only for the mom.

Lucky her.

After all of the long walks down the hallway, after the hours of back labor, after a few final pushes, we finally met our first child. I remember a friend of ours who had two kids at the time describing delivery to us. I asked her about what it was like, and without skipping a beat, she drily said, "It's like a murder scene."

Ummm...what?

"Yeah—have you ever seen one of those *CSI* shows where someone walks into a room and there's blood everywhere? It's kind of like that…"

Awkward silence.

"But it's beautiful. Because you have this kid who just popped out."

I know that, in an attempt to rationalize what you just read, you will say to yourself, "That didn't really happen. He is just trying to be funny."

As God is my witness, I promise that this is exactly how the conversation went.

So I was prepared for the worst. But when our daughter arrived into the world, I wasn't put off by the blood or the slippery glistening liquid she was covered in. I wasn't put off by the royal blue umbilical cord that extended from her belly like some sort of biological climbing rope. I was smitten. In an instant I felt a surge of bravery and courage to protect this little life from anything that would hurt her while at the same time also feeling a profound sense of weakness and helplessness, knowing that I could never do that. I looked into my wife's eyes and smiled. I looked into my daughter's eyes and smiled, too. And through all of this, I felt a desire to *speak to her*. To call her by her name. To tell her that I loved her and would always love her. To tell her *thank you* for making me a father.

When the nurses whisked her away to do their initial tests, I followed them over to their scale. By this time, our daughter was crying. Loudly. Apparently the cold hands touching her, coupled with the absence of warmth from her mom's belly, and the presence of several bright lights, sparked a reaction. She didn't like any of this. As she let out her cries, I again felt moved to speak to her. I told her that she did a great job being born. I assured her that she would get to go back to her momma soon. I tried to comfort her with my voice—with something familiar in the midst of such disorienting strangeness.

None of this makes any rational sense. Newborn babies can't understand anything that we adults say. Scientists and psychologists who study early childhood development agree that babies have no idea what adults are saying to them. They do recognize tone, but not specific words and definitely not sentences or complex ideas. So why do we speak to them? Why did I feel such compulsion to speak to my little girl in the first few minutes of her life outside the womb?

I spoke to my daughter because I wanted her to know *I was there.* Regardless of her ability to understand my specific words or intentions, I wanted her to know that she wasn't alone. That there was someone with her in the midst of all this confusion. That there was someone watching out for her even if she felt afraid or disoriented or even abandoned.

This is what prayer is like. Or this is what prayer *could* be like. Life can be incredibly confusing. We aren't always sure whom we are supposed to marry, which career we are supposed to choose, where we are supposed to live, how we are supposed to parent our kids. And we often feel discouraged by life's lack of clarity. Sometimes this discouragement leads to a deeper feeling of abandonment. Maybe God has left us to our own devices to try and navigate the complexity of our lives? But prayer has a power to remind us that we aren't alone. That there is someone with us in the midst of our confusion. That someone is watching out for us when we feel afraid or disoriented or abandoned. For the same reasons that I wanted my daughter to hear my voice, God wants us to hear his voice. This is one of the greatest comforts we can hope to experience in prayer.

Is this how you see prayer?

Most of us, whether we consider ourselves Christians or not, know how to talk to God. We know how to ask for his help, how to express some form of gratitude for his gifts to us, even how to blame him for our trials and sufferings. Talking to God in these ways—in any way, actually—is really important. And we shouldn't make that more complicated than it needs to be. He hears us. And his hearing of us is not dependent on our ability to use the right words or emotions when we convey our message to him.

But if we want to grow in our relationship with him, there are parts of our souls that need to be trained. Or maybe *developed* is the better word here. We have things inside us that want to come out in our times of communication with God. But we don't always know how to let them out in a way that builds our intimacy with God, instead of threatening it.

This is where the importance of listening comes in. Even greater than our desire to speak to God is God's desire to speak to us. Remember what the first few paragraphs in the Bible tell us—that whatever else God is, he is a God who speaks. Or in other words, he has things he wants to say.

We are fortunate that he made us with the capacity to hear him. Beyond our physical ears, God created us with a nonphysical identity called a soul, or sometimes called a "heart." This nonphysical part of who we are comes hardwired for connection with our divine Creator. And the way that we best learn how to speak *to* him is to first be spoken to *by* him.

Which makes listening in our prayers of vital importance. If we want to grow in our ability to speak with God, we have to grow in our capacity to hear from him. We are certainly free to talk with him anytime we want to. But a deeper experience of prayer comes when we learn to listen. It is in this act of listening to him, sometimes even before we speak to him, that we find out what God wants to say to us, and also how he wants us to answer him in return.

Psalms 61 and 62 are two of my favorites. I love them for what they say, but also for where they are in the Bible. This might seem obvious to most of us, but Psalm 62 comes after Psalm 61. It is entirely possible that this was a random decision made by the compiler of the Psalms. Or, and as I believe, God intentionally put these two Psalms next to each other to subtly tell us something about the nature of prayer.

Psalm 61 opens with this powerful request:

Hear my cry, O God,
listen to my prayer;
from the end of the earth I call to you
when my heart is faint.

David, the author of this Psalm, begins his prayer with an almost desperate cry out to God—"Hear me! Listen to me! I'm calling to you!" We get a little more information about the nature of this cry when he writes, "...my heart is faint." He continues:

Lead me to the rock
that is higher than I,
for you have been my refuge,
a strong tower against the enemy.
Let me dwell in your tent forever!
Let me take refuge under the shelter of your wings!

He asks to be led to a high rock, which was a sign of power and protection. He reminds his heart—and God—that God is his refuge and a "strong tower" against his enemies. Clearly David is writing from a place of insecurity, fear, and maybe even panic. He is facing things that he cannot overcome. And he needs God to intervene.

When we encounter situations that are too big for us, it is right and good that we cry out to God. In times of trauma, we don't need to overanalyze our words to him. We can just start talking to him, asking him to do things for us. We can ask him for shelter and protection and even victory over our enemies. One of the main points of Psalm 61 is that we can go to God in prayer with our side of the conversation taking priority. We can cry out to him like a child cries out for help from a parent.

But there is another side to prayer. Psalm 62, which obviously comes just after Psalm 61, tells us about a different way to encounter God's presence. This time, David writes:

For God alone my soul waits in silence;
from him comes my salvation.
He alone is my rock and my salvation,
my fortress; I shall not be greatly shaken.

Whereas Psalm 61 opens with a cry out to God, Psalm 62 begins with the opposite: *silence*. David reiterates this theme a few verses later:

> For God alone, O my soul, wait in silence,
> for my hope is from him.
> He only is my rock and my salvation,
> my fortress; I shall not be shaken.
> On God rests my salvation and my glory;
> my mighty rock, my refuge is God.

At first, David describes what his soul is doing—waiting in silence. But in the space of a few verses, his description becomes a command—"O my soul, wait in silence." He was seemingly unable to remain in this place of silence, in this posture of listening for God to speak.

We get a glimpse of what is going on in David's heart when he writes these words, which are sandwiched between these two passages:

> How long will all of you attack a man to batter him,
> like a leaning wall, a tottering fence?
> They only plan to thrust him down from his high position.
> They take pleasure in falsehood.
> They bless with their mouths, but inwardly they curse.

At first, David is waiting in silence, but something interrupts all of this. He starts to question what is happening to him, maybe even complain about it. And he informs God about what he is up against.

None of this is wrong at all. Even though God knows about our situations with far greater clarity and insight than we do, he invites us to talk to him about them. This is the foundation of intimacy—to be able to share who you are and know that you are valued and known. But David picks up on an important aspect of intimacy that we all would do well to remember. There is a time for talking, but there is also a time for listening.

Almost in mid-course of his complaint, David corrects himself by reminding his heart that, more important than being heard *by* God (at least in this instance), what he needs is to hear *from* God. This isn't easy to do. We often want to speak instead of to listen. And perhaps this is why David's tone takes a subtle shift toward a command. He has to remind his own heart that what he really needs is to wait in silence for God to speak.

And then look what happens. David starts his time with God by listening, moves to complaining, then back to listening. After a time of listening, something shifts in his heart. He sees things differently. We get no indication that God has changed David's circumstances. But he has changed David.

> Once God has spoken;
> twice have I heard this:
> that power belongs to God,
> and that to you, O Lord, belongs steadfast love.
> For you will render to a man
> according to his work.

David's anxiety is gone. David's self-pity and complaining are gone. Because David listened for God and heard him speak, he now moves out into his situation with a strengthened soul. He knows that real power belongs to God, not his enemies. He knows that no matter what happens, he still has God's love. And he knows that God will, eventually, realign every unfair situation into justice.

None of these revelations came into David's heart by speaking.

They came by listening.

These two Psalms show us the two sides of communication with God. We certainly get to talk to God in prayer. But we also get to listen. We get to hear about who he is, how he works, how he loves. I'm not going to say that one of these aspects is more important than the other. We need both. But I will say that if we are going to privilege one over the other, we should start with listening for God. Probably a lot more than we currently do.

When we make attempts to listen for God, and then when we actually *do* hear his words to us, we learn two important lessons that our hearts desperately need. First, like a child learning how to speak by being spoken to, we learn how to speak back to God in a way that builds intimacy. And the second thing we learn is that God is actually present with us, in our prayers. He is there. Even if life is confusing, even if we feel abandoned, even if we can't quite make out *everything* that he is saying to us, we can leave our times of prayer with an assurance that we are not alone—a tone of his voice that lets us know we are going to be okay.

Creating space to listen within our times of prayer is full

of difficulties. It's not easy to restrain our desire to be heard in exchange for something that seems passive and, at times, unproductive. When we speak, we are in control. When we listen, we have to surrender our control to someone else.

And then there is the problem of silence in general. Most of our world today is full of noise. Sometimes it is literal noise such as music or TV or traffic or a crying kid. Other times it's not actual sound waves hitting our eardrums, but it is the never-ending in-box, the hyperlinked articles that lead us down an Internet abyss, even the inner critic that speaks to us about how we aren't doing things well enough.

If we are going to make any progress in our ability to listen for God, we have to confront these challenges. Silence doesn't come naturally. Our desire to control runs deep. And our discomfort with stillness isn't easily defeated. But if we want to have any hope of hearing from God, it is essential that we learn how to cultivate both of these—the restraint of our words and the regular practice of stillness.

But how do we do all of this?

In regard to restraining our words, Luke tells us a story that I think is helpful. (See Luke 1.) Before Jesus was born, there was a priest named Zechariah. He was married to a woman named Elizabeth. We don't know a lot about either of these two people, but we do know that they didn't have any kids and that had to do with Elizabeth's barrenness and now their old age. And we also know that Zechariah asked God to give them a child.

One day Zechariah was fulfilling his priestly duties in the temple. During his shift, something amazing happened.

An angel appeared and told Zechariah that God had heard his prayers and was going to answer them. Elizabeth would become pregnant and give birth to a son. Not just any son, but a special son that they were to name "John." John would play a special role in preparing the world for a greater son, Jesus. He would live a unique life, spent mostly in the desert, eating bugs and honey. But he would also preach a message of repentance and hope, as well as baptize people into a new understanding of God's grace and love.

If this story isn't weird enough, this is where it gets a bit weirder. Luke tells us that Zechariah was afraid of the angel—who wouldn't be?—and even after he heard the promise of a special son, still didn't believe what the angel told him would actually happen. Something about Zechariah's fear and unbelief created a consequence: the angel struck Zechariah silent and made him unable to speak until the birth of his son. Zechariah emerged from the temple and, through unspoken signs, clued Elizabeth in to what he'd experienced. Several months later, she gave birth to their son, which she and Zechariah named John, just like the angel told them to. And immediately Zechariah could speak again.

In full disclosure, this is one of the parts of the Bible that troubles me. I think about Zechariah and how I would have responded in the same way that he did. If I saw an angel, I would be afraid. Mainly because I know enough about what the Bible says about angels to know they are not these cute and cuddly things that flutter around from cloud to cloud with harps and bows and arrows made of hearts. The Bible speaks of angels as large, booming creatures full of wings and weapons and ready to make war. And never mind the whole "How did you get in my room?" factor, too. Fear, to me, seems like a natural response. And if I were advanced in years (translation: I wake up five times a night to go to bathroom because I'm O-L-D) and someone told me that I was going to have a child, I would probably doubt that prediction, too. Zechariah seems to respond in a very normal, human way. But God, through his angel, strikes him with an inability to speak because of his response. While this seems harsh to me, I'm obviously not God and he has his reasons—which, I'm sure, are far beyond my ability to comprehend.

While I don't understand why God does this, I can see the good in it. Whatever we know about Zechariah, we can safely say that he had ideas and desires about how his life should go. He even talked to God about these desires, asking God to give his wife the gift of pregnancy and the birth of a child.

I don't want to project too many things onto poor Zechariah, but I can only speak from a little bit of my experience here. When my wife and I wanted to start a family, things did not unfold on the timetable that we expected. We assumed that pregnancy and birth would come easily. It didn't. Thankfully we now have the joy of parenting four beautiful children, but I remember the almost two years we endured before our first pregnancy. It was hard. We cried out to God for his help. And we also met with doctors and took tests and tried to do whatever we needed to do on our end to make something happen. Throughout all of this, God surfaced this idea of control in both of our hearts. This was a long and complicated realization that would deserve a book of its own, but the short story is my wife and I realized that we had put God in a box. This box was built with our wooden expectations. When God didn't meet our expectations, we clung to our sense of control. When that didn't work, we had to face the God who was disappointing us in new, powerful ways. And we emerged from this experience with a resignation to his will and a deeper trust in his timing. But all of this took a painful surrender of our control. In some ways, it took us saying that we wouldn't speak to God about what we thought he *should do*, but instead try, many times with weak and feeble hearts, to listen for God and what he *was doing*.

One of the greatest paradoxes of our human existence is the illusion of control. God gives us a tremendous amount of freedom to exercise our choices, our preferences. But he remains in control of everything. I don't know how all of this works, but I do know that I live in this paradox daily. Because of my limited freedom, I think that I have real control of my life. But then something happens—a surge of traffic, an unexpected tax bill, a babysitter cancels—and I realize that I am actually in control of very little in my life.

After a few decades of walking with Jesus, here is what I know: God sometimes limits our freedoms in order to drive this truth into our hearts. He is in control. We are not.

Full stop.

I think this is what's happening with Zechariah. Zechariah thought he was in control of his life. When the angel showed up and reminded Zechariah that God was the one who was in control of his life, there was something in Zechariah that didn't want to surrender to this. To yield. God is a god who will have his way. In an effort to drive this truth into Zechariah's heart, he struck him silent and made him unable to speak. Maybe just to remind Zechariah that he was under someone else's orders.

When we cultivate silence in our lives, specifically in our prayers, we remind our own hearts of this same thing. While we feel a great burden to express our thoughts and desires to God through our words, sometimes what we most need is to remember that we are under someone else. He is the King. He is the one with real control. We can have our plans and hopes of how things should go, but ultimately those need to fall under a greater set of plans, a greater understanding.

God is a master builder. He sees past, present, and future all at once. He lovingly and graciously weaves together *every moment of the entire universe*. When we choose to silence our hearts and listen to God, we are saying to him that we yield to his plans, his voice. It's vitally important that we listen to what he has to say.

Even if we do all of this—even if we surrender our control and choose to sit in silence before God—how do we keep our hearts and minds and bodies in a posture of stillness to hear from him? How do we quiet our fractured, distracted attention spans long enough to hear what he has to say to us?

Again, this isn't easy. Most of our modern world steers us toward anything—*everything*—but stillness. So we need to realize what we're up against. But it is possible. Here are a few practices that I have found helpful:

First, make solitude a priority. Our hearts were meant to share connections with other people. There is no getting around the fact that we need relationships with people in order to be healthy human beings. There are several major medical studies that confirm the danger of isolation and loneliness and the harmful effects they have on our physical and emotional health. But I'm not talking about isolating ourselves from others or persisting in patterns of loneliness and disconnection.

When I talk about solitude, I'm talking about intentional times away from people for the sake of spiritual growth. I once heard someone say that when he spent time alone, he wasn't spending time *by* himself. He was spending time *with* his self. This is a good way to think about solitude. Our hearts are quiet creatures, forged in the background of our daily lives. Sometimes they will shout to us over the persistent noise of our families, our jobs, our responsibilities, our fears, our worries. But they mostly remain hidden, and quiet. They prefer to whisper instead of shout. When we pull away from others in an effort to spend time with ourselves, we give our hearts a chance to speak to us. To tell us how we are really doing.

It is in these times that we are primed to hear God speak to us, as well. God certainly does—and can—speak to us audibly. But it has been my experience—and countless others, as well—that God more often speaks to us through impressions or thoughts that "come out of nowhere." He speaks to us with a gentleness, even a smallness. Spending time in intentional solitude enables us to hear him in his smallness, free from the distractions and noise of our daily grind.

Second, slow down in prayer, in order to hear God's voice. Have you ever noticed that Jesus was never in a hurry? Even when his friend Lazarus was dying, Jesus took his time, arriving four days (seemingly) too late. Another time, someone told

Jesus that a leader's daughter was sick and about to die. She needed urgent help. Jesus agreed to go to her, but somewhere along the way an old woman touched his clothes, and in an act of superhuman perception, Jesus became aware that "power had gone out of him." Instead of telling this woman that he had just been summoned to heal a dying girl, Jesus paused and talked with her. You can imagine the nervousness of his handler at this point:

"Jesus, I'm not trying to be rude here but this old woman has been sick for twelve years. A few more hours won't hurt. And, besides, she is old. She has most of her life behind her. We need to get going NOW because there is a little girl—the little girl that you agreed to help—who is getting worse by the minute. And she has her whole life ahead of her. You having this conversation might be her death warrant. Come on, let's get out of here."

Of course, Jesus knew all of this. But still he patiently took his time. He ended up healing the older woman who'd touched his clothes, then made his way to the little girl and healed her, too.

Jesus never hurried. When crowds followed him with their needs, Jesus would interact with them for a while—sometimes a long while—but then he would routinely pull away for times of solitude and prayer. Leaving a lot undone, I might add.

Our lives move fast. Sometimes I think about my grandparents and how they have literally seen the dawn of modern technology. When they were born, meals took hours to prepare. Now they can microwave popcorn in two minutes. Traveling to another state used to take them hours, even days. Now they can board a jet and cover the *entire country* in less time than it takes to watch two movies. In generations past, a woman who gave birth to a child used to be in the hospital for a week, maybe more. Now, thanks to our advancements in medicine and surgery, she could be home after just a few days. And think about this last one: if my grandparents wanted to know who won the World Series in 1912, they would have had to either call someone who knew these sorts of things or look it up in a book they had at home or, even worse, go to a library and search for a book that had this information in it (with the Dewey Decimal System and a card catalog). All of these would take time. Now they can type a few words into their spaceship-phone-computer-camera thingy and get the answer in less than a second.

Incredible.

It's almost unbelievable to think about some of this. And for those of us who came into this world with technology—and the speed it produces—in full force, we don't know anything else. Our hearts grow up with hurry as their longtime partner and friend. With all of its advantages, though, our modern world has created an unintended consequence. We can't slow down. Even in our spiritual lives and interactions with God through prayer, we bring this hurried state into our conversations with him. We might ask God to speak to us, but then we find ourselves unwilling to stick around to hear him answer because we simply can't sit still, can't quiet our hearts, can't ignore the text messages coming in to our phones.

John Ortberg, who is a pastor and author, was once talking with Dallas Willard, who was a professor and author, about how to experience Jesus more deeply. By this time, Willard had written much about spiritual growth, the Kingdom of God, and how we can make progress in both of these. Ortberg, by his own admission, expected his wiser and older friend to say something deep and profound. Willard obliged, but not in the way Ortberg expected. Willard simply said, "You must eliminate all forms of hurry in your life."

These are wise words. And we would all do well to heed them. Imagine sitting down with an old childhood friend that you haven't seen for several years. Since you last saw each other, both of you have gotten married, had kids, changed jobs, suffered. In an act of graciousness, he forgoes his desire to share the events of his life that you have missed and instead asks you about your life. You appreciate the opportunity to open up, so you start to share. At first your friend seems to listen, but after a few minutes he starts to fidget. He looks around the room at everything else that is going on. He checks his watch. He checks his phone. And then he says, "Hey, it's great to see you...but would you mind hurrying up a bit? I've got a really busy day and I need to get moving."

There is simply no way that the two of you can experience intimacy or meaningful communication underneath a tone of hurry.

How often do we do this with God?

We hurry through our times of prayer, virtually eliminating any possibility of hearing him speak to us, for no other reason except we are too hurried to hear his voice.

God is a speaking God. Hearing him is often hard, mainly

because we don't like to be alone with our hearts and we don't like to slow down. But if prayer is, at its most basic level, a relationship with God, that means our communication isn't one-way. We get to speak to him about our lives and concerns and desires. But God wants to speak to us, too.

If we would only listen.

10 AWARENESS

THERE ARE PARTS of the Bible that trouble me. My troubles usually fall into two categories: either I don't understand something that I read, or—and this is the more troubling of the two—I *do* understand what I read, but I can't seem to bring it into my life in a meaningful way. Or at least in a way that I think will please God.

When Jesus says that we are supposed to love our enemies, this is what I'm talking about. I understand what he means. But bringing it into my life? That's a harder and longer road. I can vaguely grab on to the idea when I think about someone like Hitler or Stalin or Jeffrey Dahmer or any other especially evil person that I can pull out of history. Something about these kinds of enemies, because of their grandiosity and their sheer evilness, rouses in me something that resembles nobility. I feel like it is noble to extend mercy and grace and love to such deplorable people. The greater their evil, the more noble my act of love becomes.

Of course, this is an illusion of my heart's own making. I can imagine loving these kinds of enemies because they have never hurt *me*. The call to love them doesn't register as a personal sacrifice because they haven't taken anything from me. They haven't murdered *my* uncle. They haven't enslaved *my* family. They haven't violated *my* boundaries.

But the second an enemy becomes personal, I have trouble. The coworker who gossips about me behind my back, with venomous lies. The police officer who gives me a ticket for a minor speeding offense, for no good reason. The white Honda in the left lane on the highway who drives five miles under the speed limit, which is the *exact* speed as the semi-truck next to it, for several miles, making me late to my meeting. The family members who put their needs and wants ahead of mine.

When your enemies are close to you, that's where Jesus' words start to sting. Loving an enemy that is distant and impersonal isn't easy, but it is at least free of one main hazard: you don't have to see them very often. But what do you do when one of your own family members, when one of your coworkers, when one of your neighbors legitimately acts like one of your enemies? And you are forced by geography alone to face hurt and pain and conflict with them? Sometimes daily. Sometimes hourly.

This is where I have trouble with Jesus' words.

Loving your enemies is hard when they are consistently three feet away from you.

Another part of the Bible that I have trouble with comes in Paul's first letter to the Thessalonians. As he wraps things up, he gives his readers this simple instruction in 5:27: *pray without ceasing*. I can't remember when I first heard about this command, but I know it was very early in my journey with Jesus.

I heard Christians whom I respected and admired often cite these words as they described their personal habits of prayer. I also remember that, as soon as I heard them talk about Paul's instruction, I immediately felt disqualified.

How could I pray *without ceasing?* I wasn't sure, but I had visions of what this meant. A slightly disheveled man in a beard and a robe, holed up in a cave somewhere, praying. His knees are worn smooth from kneeling. His eyes can't help but squint in the sun because they are usually clenched closed, in prayer. His voice is soft and it almost surprises him to hear it when it leaks out of his mouth because he is more comfortable with silence than he is with speaking. He doesn't like visitors. They are interruptions. And he definitely doesn't like small talk, either. Who cares about such silliness as the weather when he could be talking about God? Or better yet, talking *to* God? He wakes up before the sun comes out, and he prays. He spends all day praying. He stays up late into the dark evening, praying. Sometime in the night, he sleeps. Somehow he mysteriously eats. But all of these are burdens to endure, not gifts to enjoy. His real purpose in life is to pray. Everything else is a secondary distraction. Maybe even a sinful distraction.

I know how absurd this sounds, but this is what I honestly thought when I heard Paul's words. I thought that true spirituality consisted of a retreat from the world around me—how else could I pray all the time? In my mind, I created a (false) division between normal life and spiritual life. Normal life consisted of eating and drinking and sleeping and checking my e-mail and going to the grocery store and mowing the lawn and watching football on Sunday afternoons. Spiritual life, however, consisted of reading the Bible and praying and going to church and…that was mostly it. Maybe listening to Christian music, too. But only if I wasn't doing anything else at the time.

In my mind, this dichotomy led to a binary existence. Either I was doing "worldly" things or I was doing "godly" things. And these two spheres didn't intersect. The task of the Christian, then, was to do as few worldly things as possible—just enough to survive—while trying as hard as possible to pull away for spiritual things instead.

This distinction between sacred and secular is harmful to a soul on many levels. And it's not a biblical understanding of how God interacts with his world and, consequently, how he desires his followers to interact with his world, either. But this is what I did. Quite often.

When I divided the world into these two sections of "worldly" and "spiritual"—or more truthfully, "God" and "Not God"—I put into place a line that ran through everything in my life. Playing golf with my dad? Not God. Going to church? God. Waiting tables on a Friday night at work? Not God. Going to early morning prayer with a friend from Bible study? God. Watching an R-rated movie? Definitely Not God. Reading a commentary about Luke's Gospel? Definitely God.

Categorizing the world this way led me to feel a tremendous amount of uncertainty. I wanted to go to church. But I had all these desires to live a normal, human life, too. I wanted to read the Bible. But I also wanted to watch movies and listen to music and read books that weren't about Jesus at all. I wanted to be a committed follower of God, for sure. But I also wanted to be a photographer. Or maybe an architect. Or a writer.

Sometimes I felt guilty for these things, but mostly I just felt unsteadied by them. When I read Paul's words about praying without ceasing, I took that to mean that God's standard for my life was to live constantly in prayer. Anything less than that was disappointing to him. I didn't have the scorecard entirely worked out, but I figured that God made allowances for doing the things that I *had* to do. I didn't think he was disappointed in me for going to school or going to work or brushing my teeth— thank God. But I did feel a low-grade uncertainty around nearly everything else. *How could I justify watching three hours of TV when there was so much prayer to pray?*

Continuing with my black-and-white thinking, I figured I had two options. Either I could soften Paul's words by telling myself that he didn't mean what I thought he meant, or at the very least that he was using hyperbole to convey his point. He didn't *really* mean that we were supposed to pray all the time. Or I could soften my responsibility to his words by telling myself that, even though Paul did mean what I thought he meant, there was no way I could come close to experiencing that kind of a prayer life. So I might as well just accept that I was destined to be on the B-Team of prayer and get on with my normal, mostly unspiritual life. And hopefully God would understand.

As I grew in my faith, I realized that neither of these were good options. If I was going to soften Paul's words, then where did that end? There were a lot of other parts of the Bible that

I wanted to soften, as well. Pray for my enemies? God didn't really mean that. Keep sex pure by saving it for the covenant of marriage? Nope. Definitely not what God meant. Give generously to a local church? No on that, too. Slowly, but surely, the slope became too slippery. If I kept on this trajectory of softening God's teachings, then my faith would lose its teeth. It would lose its conviction. Its power.

So that was out.

And when I tried to soften my responsibility to these words and simply accept the fact that I wasn't going to be a "strong" Christian, that didn't work, either. One of the foundational beliefs in the gospel message is that no one is better than anyone else. It is by grace alone that we are saved. And this grace comes with a fullness that God designed to change us, deeply. If we are surrendering to Jesus as a King, then we are either under his authority and power or we aren't. There is no middle ground. To live in his Kingdom, with him as our King, means that we can't avoid our responsibilities (and joys) of obedience to his will and ways.

So that was out, too.

I confess that this idea of praying all the time remained a mystery to me for several years. I simply didn't know how to make it work in my life. Until I read two books that changed my perspective, hopefully forever.

The first book is by a man named Nicholas Herman. We don't know a lot about Nicholas. He lived in the seventeenth century, in France. He grew up very poor. When he was older, he joined the army, mainly because of the guarantee of food and shelter. During his time in the army, he had a spiritual experience of God's love that left him deeply moved. He was later injured while serving as a soldier, upon which he retired from the army. With his commitment to the army no longer anchoring his vocational life, Nicholas sought out a place to grow in his understanding of God's love further. He chose to enter a monastery in Paris as a monk. As was the custom when someone entered into religious orders, he received a new name: Brother Lawrence.

Whether because of his war-related injury or his relatively new status as a monk, Brother Lawrence's superiors assigned him the inglorious job of kitchen duty. This meant that Brother Lawrence was responsible for cooking and preparing meals for the other monks, as well as cleaning up the pots and pans after the meals. The work was humbling. It was tedious, routine, and we can only guess, boring.

But it was also the work of God.

As Brother Lawrence adjusted to his role in the kitchen, God adjusted his heart in such a profound and truly magnificent way that, hundreds of years later, when I read his words, I was struck with a strong appreciation for his insights into life with God. And I don't mean "appreciation" as in "That's a really nice painting you have hanging above your fireplace." I mean "appreciation" as in "I'm standing on the lip of the Grand Canyon and the beauty of what's before my eyes is almost too much to take in." Like, there's not a big enough place in my soul to store it all. All I can do is stand there, speechless, but still searching for words. All I can do is stand there, aware that what I am witnessing is some sort of invitation to go further into beauty and mystery and God himself.

Most of what we have from Brother Lawrence comes to us through his preserved letters and "maxims," which were short teachings he (or his fellow monks whom he helped guide) wrote down—now published in what is commonly called *The Practice of the Presence of God*. You could read these letters and maxims in an afternoon. Easily. But that doesn't mean they are easy readings.

In his writings, Brother Lawrence, with unparalleled simplicity and grace, describes a kind of life with God that oozes ease. Somehow he experienced a relationship with God that tapped into what Paul was talking about—near constant communication with the divine. While Brother Lawrence prepared his meals, cleaned his pots, scrubbed his pans, he also prayed. And it was the best kind of prayer. He knew that God heard him, and he knew that he heard God. Like a hidden, behind-the-scenes dialogue, Brother Lawrence kept a kind of communion with God that was unaffected by his outer, "worldly" surroundings.

For Brother Lawrence, life did not fall into a dualist distinction of God and Not God. It was All God. Cutting the carrots, rinsing the utensils, drying the plates, communing with the God of the universe—they all happened at the same time. He didn't have to pull away from his worldly responsibilities in order to experience the God of Creation, the God of his heart. He found a way to experience God's grace *through* his worldly responsibilities.

It's not worth summarizing his teachings here—I would only water down what is meant to be sipped neat. You can read them for yourself. But perhaps one thought is worth sharing, when Brother Lawrence writes,

> The Lord does not really lay any great burden on us. He only wants you to recall Him to mind as often as possible, to pour out your adoration on Him, to pray for His grace. Offer him your sorrows. Return from time to time to Him, and quietly, purely thank Him for the benefit He has given you in knowing Him. Thank Him, too, for the benefit He pours out upon you even in the midst of your troubles. The Lord asks you to let Him be the one who consoles you, just as often as you can find it in you to come to Him.[1]

And maybe one more:

> Think often of God; do so by day and by night, in your business and even during diversions. The Lord is always near you. He is with you. For your part, never leave him alone.[2]

For Brother Lawrence, this is the entire point of a relationship with God. And of prayer, too. That God is *near*. He is around us all the time. We don't need to escape the lives around us in order to find him. He is near to us in everything that we encounter throughout our days. Prayer, then, consists of "taking solace in him" and "lifting up our hearts to him," wherever we are, whatever we are doing.

Maybe a helpful way to think about prayer is simply this: *we refuse to leave God alone.* Because he has not left us alone.

Another one of God's followers found these same truths. In the early part of the twentieth century, Frank Laubach and his wife moved to the Philippines to live as missionaries. He founded several churches and even a college. He taught thousands of people how to read and write. But his greatest contribution—at least to me—is his writings on prayer.

Like so many pastors and ministers, Laubach found himself in this paradox. He was doing God's work, but he struggled to sense God's work in himself. Resolved to discover a new way forward, a way in which he could experience God's work in his heart while he was performing God's work outside of it, Laubach came up with a new way to live. In his own words, here is how he describes his "experiment":

> For the past few days I have been experimenting in a more complete surrender than ever before. I am taking by deliberate act of will, enough time from each hour to give God much thought. Yesterday and today I have made a new adventure, which is not easy to express. I am feeling God in each movement, by an act of will— willing that He shall direct these fingers that now strike this typewriter—willing that He shall pour through my steps as I walk—willing that He shall direct my words as I speak, and my very jaws as I eat![3]

For Laubach, he set his heart to experience God's "movement" through his many, seemingly mundane movements throughout his day. And this is what he began to feel:

> I feel simply carried along each hour, doing my part in a plan which is far beyond myself. This sense of cooperation with God in the little things is what astonishes me. I seem to have to make sure of only one thing now, and every other thing "takes care of itself," or I prefer to say what is more true, God takes care of all the rest. My part is to live in this hour in continuous inner conversation with God and in perfect responsiveness to His will. To make this hour gloriously rich. This seems to be all I need to think about.[4]

I love that image—of being "carried along each hour" by God himself. For Laubach, this increased awareness of God through this quiet, hidden practice of prayer reminded his heart of its true place within God's Kingdom. God does the work. We do not. Our part is simply to respond to God's work. And this rhythm of God working and us responding creates in us a feeling of being "gloriously rich" in God's presence.

When I read these words many years ago, I felt the same thing I felt when I first looked over the Grand Canyon. I felt like I was staring at something very, very large. Very mysterious. Very powerful. And I felt appropriately small. I felt appropriately poor. But I also felt invited into a life of glorious richness.

For Brother Lawrence and for Frank Laubach, the method

was the same. They both related to God as someone who is always with us. Prayer consists primarily of remembering this truth. God is always there, always *here*. He wants us to notice him through the small act of turning our heart's attention toward him.

This can look different for different personalities and even seasons of life, but the principle remains the same. We try to keep two things in our minds and hearts at once. On the one hand, we do what is in front of us: We clean the dishes. We give our kids a bath. We pay our bills. We sit in traffic. But on the other hand, we remember what is around us—namely, God himself. So while we are doing the things that are in front of us, we are also connecting with the God who is around us and around all the things we are doing. He is there with us in the kitchen. He is there with us in the cubicle. He is there with us when we exchange a small courtesy of words with the person behind the counter making our sandwich for our lunch.

While this is simple, we can't pretend all of it is easy. It's hard to remember *to remember* something. It's even harder to remember to be aware of something that is all around us, that we can easily take for granted. If God is everywhere, that means he is familiar. Meaning, we can become so accustomed to his presence that we end up ignoring it. Think about the reality of air. It surrounds you all the time, but how often do you really live with an awareness of oxygen passing into and back out of your lungs?

David Foster Wallace describes the challenge in living with an awareness of what is around us in his now-famous graduation-speech-turned-book *This Is Water*. He humorously opens his speech with these words:

> There are these two young fish swimming along, and they happen to meet an older fish swimming the other way, who nods at them and says, "Morning, boys, how's the water?" And the two young fish swim on for a bit, and then eventually one of them looks over at the other and goes, "What the hell is water?"

Wallace quickly explains his point when he says:

> If at this moment, you're worried that I plan to present myself here as the wise old fish explaining what water is to you younger fish, please don't be. I am not the wise old fish. The immediate point of the fish story is that the most obvious, ubiquitous, important realities are often the ones that are the hardest to see and talk about.[5]

Yes.

And Amen.

If God is the Creator of our world and all that is in it, he is most surely "the most obvious, ubiquitous, important" reality. But because he is so obvious, because he is so ubiquitous, he is often very hard to see and talk about. Because we so easily take his presence for granted.

This is one of the greatest challenges and, consequently, invitations of prayer. God is everywhere. But because he is everywhere, we end up treating him as if he were nowhere. We don't sense in our hearts a separation between what is God and what is Not God, so we end up living as if most of our lives were full of Not God. Which explains why we don't pray very often. Or even when we do pray, it feels labored and artificial and like we are going through a few, religiously inspired motions.

There is a different way. Prayer can be more than motions. It can be life. And power. And compassion. And love.

When my wife and I first started dating, I wanted to impress her. Since high school, I have had a relatively fast metabolism. Coupled with my relatively tall height, you get someone who is considered slim. Or in other respects, *gangly*. So taking off my shirt and flexing was off the table. But I really wanted her to like me. So I tried to impress her in other ways.

One night I invited her over for dinner. I found a recipe for an Italian dish that even called for red wine in it. I planned everything out so that when she arrived, the dinner would only be half-finished. It was important that she was in the kitchen when I poured the wine into the sauce so she could see how sophisticated this man in front of her actually was.

Impressive, right?

So she arrived and there we were, standing in the kitchen. I poured in the wine. She barely noticed.

I was crestfallen. I finished the dish, fixed the salad, lit the candle—all the usual things that go into a date like this. We sat down at the table and, thankfully, enjoyed the night together. We laughed and talked and laughed some more. We shared dreams. We smiled at each other. We began to let each other in.

As all of this was happening, I realized that the wine in the dish didn't matter. The candle didn't matter. The playlist didn't matter. None of it did. Every effort I'd made to create a perfect evening was empty until something else filled it. Every motion I went through would remain false and forced until other, more important things like love and grace and joy and peace entered into our time together. Then, once those were present, we had the real things I was after. Intimacy. Being known. Affection. Compassion.

These are things that God wants to inject into our daily lives. His life. His power. His compassion. His love. That's his part in all of this—he is the rich man who wants to share his wealth with his kids. Our part is simply to acknowledge him as the rich man and then to open our hands as both a sign of surrender and a sign that we want to receive whatever riches he wants to share with us.

There is never a place in our lives where God isn't rich. There is never a time in our lives when God doesn't want to share his richness with us. And we don't have to retreat into a cave in order to experience God's richness toward us. It is always with us. *He* is always with us. What God wants from us is not a dramatic withdrawal from the lives around us, but instead a dramatic awareness of his presence *within* the lives around us.

I think this is what Paul is talking about when he writes that we are supposed to pray "without ceasing." For Paul, Jesus truly was *all*. He found Jesus in the bread and wine of Communion. But he also found Jesus in the mist of the open sea, the dust of the open road. He found Jesus in the gathering of the saints, but he also found Jesus in the gathering of his friends. Paul knew, in what appears to be an unshakable way, that he lived his life within God's grand world. And part of knowing God meant that Paul was able to know this God within the world around him. Vividly.

Sitting at the kitchen table with your daughter.

God, you're here with me. What do you want me to hear in this moment?

Driving to work in your car.

God, you're here with me. How can I respond to you in this moment?

Confronting an enemy, and trying to love him.

God, you're here with me. Is there anything I need to be aware of in this moment?

Celebrating your wife or husband on a date.

God, you're here with me. How can I show you gratitude in this moment?

Lying in a hospital bed, waiting for death to come.

God, you're here with me. Help me to see you in this moment.

Unceasing prayer.

In all.

And through all.

Because God can be found in all.

Every minute.

11 REPENTANCE

WHENEVER WE PRAY, we are dealing with God. This should seem rather obvious, but it's amazing how hard it is for me to keep this simple, foundational belief as a firm, steadying fixture in my heart. This belief contains a few simple, foundational implications that our hearts need to remember.

First, if we are going to risk belief in a god, we might as well go the whole way and risk a belief in a God—with a capital "G." Meaning, if we are going to put our hearts and lives in front of a divine being, shouldn't this divine being be the kind of god who sits over everything we are bringing to him? Shouldn't this divine being possess the power and authority to actually change things in our lives? Shouldn't this divine being be so far above and beyond our own power and authority— and above and beyond *all* powers and authorities—that there is literally nothing that he can't do?

Yes.

Praying to any other type of god is an exercise in futility. Unlike the ancient Greeks and Romans, we don't have a hierarchy of gods who act in random, even selfish ways. We have

God. There is nothing above him that makes him do anything, for he is all-powerful. There is nothing beside him that makes him an equal to anyone or anything. There is nothing below him over which he cannot rule. He is *God*.

If this first implication is true—which I think it is—then a second implication follows. The only kind of God who could exist in such total power and absolute sovereignty (which means he has complete freedom to do whatever he wants to do) would be so utterly different and beyond me. Imagine a grain of sand. Now imagine Mount Everest. Now put that grain of sand next to Mount Everest. And now use your mind's eye to grow Mount Everest about a thousand times—so high that it stretches out into space and almost touches the moon.

This exercise in visualization is but a mere attempt to portray the gap that exists between us and God. He is like the greatest of mountains. *Unreasonably* great. And we are like the smallest of grains of sand. When you put these two things next to each other, the juxtaposition should make something very clear: God is so much different than we are.

A third implication follows, then. If we are not going to settle for belief in a god, but instead believe in God himself, and we realize that we are not like this God that we are believing in and talking with, then we have to ask what makes us different from this God? Apart from power and size and all the other usual things we associate with divine beings, is there anything else that distinguishes God from ourselves?

The answer is that there are a lot of things that distinguish God from us. Theologians and philosophers and artists and poets and even ancient men who lived by fires and in caves have much to tell us about the many differences that exist between us and the divine. But perhaps the simplest way to think about all these differences is by focusing on one word: *holiness*. This isn't a word that we often use today. Especially if we aren't connected to a Christian community of faith. And yet it is vital that we understand what this word means and how it impacts our relationship with God.

Holiness, in its simplest form, means perfection. I know just enough about philosophy to appear as though I understand some of its main concepts, that is, until I find myself in a conversation with an actual philosopher and then the jig is up. I am quickly exposed for the ignorant fraud that I am. But one thing I think I do understand is an idea that an ancient Greek named Plato made popular when he lived, and has since become integrated into the foundations of our Western attempts to make sense of the world.[1]

Hang with me here.

Plato felt plagued by a common problem that he witnessed everywhere, and it goes like this: No matter how hard he tried, Plato couldn't hang on to happiness. The problem with happiness is that it's fleeting—when we think we have it, something changes and it goes away. Human beings keep chasing this fleeting happiness, but as long as we live in this material world, happiness always seems to leave. Like vapor or smoke passing through our hands, we can't ever seem to grasp it, to keep it around as a steady constant in our lives.

As Plato worked on this problem, he realized that happiness avoids us because the things around us constantly change. For example, we enjoy a period of health and that makes us happy. But eventually our health fades and we find ourselves facing a sickness that makes us feel unhappy. What used to give us a sense of fulfillment and satisfaction—our health—has changed. And we no longer feel happy. Why? Because we tied our hearts to something that we expected to remain permanent, and then something happened and we instead found our hearts tied to something that changed. Naturally, disappointment, sadness, even anger and resentment follow.

All of this really bothered Plato. He wondered how human beings could ever find fulfillment or satisfaction—or what he called "happiness"—in a world like this. In a world where everything changed and left us wanting for something more.

In an attempt to solve this condition and somehow find peace for his restless heart, Plato formulated an idea. He decided that the human heart's desire for happiness—which was often determined by permanence and stability—was good. But living in a world that changes constantly leaves our hearts unhappy, because we want things to be permanent and they never are.

This is where Plato becomes important for us as we think about God and prayer.

Plato determined that we all face two realities. If our ever-changing world, filled with impermanence and instability, was all that there was, then our hearts were destined to be miserable because they would always want something that they could never have. Men and women, then, would only be able to live lives of meaninglessness. Happiness would always run away from them, like some kind of cosmic game of tag. We could chase happiness, and even grasp it sometimes, but it would never stay. We would never find lasting fulfillment and satisfaction.

Sounds horrible, right?

It sounded horrible to Plato, too. So Plato deduced that there had to be another reality. One that made his life more bearable in the face of such uncertainty and impermanence. Plato felt deeply in his heart that happiness was a good desire. He couldn't abandon it. There was something about happiness that was meant to find fulfillment. Somewhere. He knew that this world would never give him—or anyone else—the kind of fulfillment that he desired. So he concluded that there must be another world. *Somewhere.* This other world was permanent and stable and contained perfection. Our world—the changing, unstable, imperfect world—was merely a reflection of this other, better, more authentic world. Our hearts can find happiness and fulfillment when we connect to this other, perfect world and attach our happiness and sense of meaning to what we find *there*, versus what we find *here*, in our imperfect, changing world.

Plato called this other world a world of "forms," meaning that everything that exists in our world comes from a more perfect form or reality that exists somewhere else. Even though the things around us change, the perfect forms of the things around us never change.

Plato also concluded that it was enough to know that this kind of reality existed. This gave him a sense of peace (or did it?) because it freed him from placing his hopes for happiness in the changing, impermanent world around him. He knew that whatever he desired would ultimately leave him wanting because it would eventually change. All of life's promises of happiness were actually deceptions. True happiness, then, was freedom from trusting imperfect things to be perfect.

In regard to God and prayer and how our hearts can relate to both of these things, it's not important to understand the technical aspects of Plato's ideas. What is important to understand, however, is that, when faced with the two realities of a changing, impermanent, imperfect world on the one hand and a heart that desired permanence and perfection on the other, Plato didn't abandon either. He didn't settle for "The world will hurt you and suck you dry so your life is meaningless." And he didn't settle for "The world should give you everything you want so your life will be happy," either. He held both of these in his hands. An imperfect world will hurt you. But you can be happy. Because perfection exists *somewhere*. And that is enough.

C. S. Lewis says the same thing, which I already pointed to in chapter 6:

> The Christian says, "Creatures are not born with desires unless satisfaction for those desires exists. A baby feels hunger: well, there is such a thing as food. A duckling wants to swim: well, there is such a thing as water. Men feel sexual desire: well, there is such a thing as sex. If I find in myself a desire which no experience in this world can satisfy, the most probable explanation is that I was made for another world. If none of my earthly pleasures satisfy it, that does not prove that the universe is a fraud. Probably earthly pleasures were never meant to satisfy it, but only to arouse it, to suggest the

real thing. If that is so, I must take care, on the one hand, never to despise, or to be unthankful for, these earthly blessings, and on the other, never to mistake them for the something else of which they are only a kind of copy, or echo, or mirage. I must keep alive in myself the desire for my true country, which I shall not find till after death; I must never let it get snowed under or turned aside; I must make it the main object of life to press on to that country and to help others to do the same."[2]

For Lewis, our desires for happiness, permanence, and perfection are indicators that they must exist *somewhere*. If they don't exist in our current world, that doesn't mean they don't exist. It just means that there must be another world somewhere in which they do.

Prayer is where all of this connects for us and becomes real to our hearts. We want things to be perfect. They (so obviously) aren't. But we sense that they *could* be perfect somewhere. The good meal would be perfect and never end. The deep friendship would be perfect and never change. The euphoria experienced during romance would be perfect and never fade. Somewhere this kind of perfection exists. We know this to be true because, when we look at our hearts, we find the desire for this kind of world natively occupying its territory. We can't drop the desire for perfection and permanence even if we tried.

That "somewhere" is God. He is perfect. He is unchanging. He is stable. Everything that is good and right with the world that we want to remain unchanged exists in him, in fullness.

And this is what holiness means.

God lacks nothing that is good. He possesses nothing that isn't. And he never changes.

While this truth should give us a great comfort, it also creates for us a great problem. If God is perfect and unchanging and *holy*, how are we supposed to relate to him? Every human heart that has ever pumped blood, every human mind that has ever thought thoughts knows—with searing, heartbreaking clarity—that we are not perfect. We are not unchanging. We are not *holy*.

It almost isn't even worth exploring this idea any further because we know it so intimately. But just in case we need reminders, think about the stay-at-home mom (or dad) who simultaneously loves her children, but wants to put them in a boarding school—or at least in front of the TV for a few hours—because she is out of patience and is sick of their immaturity.

Imperfect.

Not holy.

Think about the corporate executive or governmental official who initially took the job to serve those around him, to make the world better. But after a few years (months?) into his new role, he realizes that he enjoys the power that his position provides. And he starts to use his position to serve not only those to whom he is responsible, but himself, as well.

Imperfect.

Not holy.

Think about the toddler who identifies his favorite toy at preschool and then proceeds to hoard it, preventing other kids from playing with it. Even when he wants to play with another toy, he can't let go of his "favorite" toy because then someone else might enjoy it and he won't be able to any longer.

Imperfect.

Not holy.

The list could go forever. Just think about your last twenty-four hours. If you're like me, or anyone really, I'm sure you have had moments where you performed a good deed, said a kind word, acted selflessly when you could have acted selfishly—you did good things. You *were* good. But you also had moments when you judged someone, when you spoke words of anger and hurt, when you took the last piece of cake in the office break room when you knew that Sheila really likes cake and was having a hard day and that would have helped ease her pain a bit, but dear God, you really wanted that cake, too, so you ate it instead of giving it to her.

Imperfect.

Not holy.

After I met my wife, Ashley, and fell in love with her, I realized that I wanted to marry her. Since I am an American male, I also realized that the money I had saved for a month-long trip through Europe would now have to be redistributed to something small and shiny and would fit on her left ring finger. I soon learned that "precious"—as in "precious metal" or "precious diamond"—was just another, more luxurious way to say "exorbitantly expensive."

The gentleman who guided me in picking out a ring was a genius. He didn't show me his best diamond at first. Instead, he showed me a stone that looked adequately nice. The price was right and the size was honestly bigger than I thought I could afford. I was ready to take it. But then, like some sort of Jedi, he said that he had one more stone he would like to show me—"just in case I liked it better."

Out came a smaller stone. He placed it on the black velvet wrap that he had laid out on the counter. He pushed it around and prodded it a bit with his poker thing and asked what I thought. I told him it looked obviously smaller than the previous stone and I wasn't interested.

"Okay—I understand. But size isn't everything. Take a look at it now."

I looked down to the black velvet wrap again and saw the smaller diamond. But this time, he had placed it next to the larger—and I might add *less expensive*—diamond and asked what I thought.

I was shocked.

When placed next to the larger stone, the smaller stone looked remarkably better. Brighter. More brilliant. More beautiful.

"Size isn't everything in a diamond. Cut, clarity—these two things actually make a stone *sing*."

He was right.

And he was about to become a bit richer, too. I did some quick math in my head, figured that I didn't have to have certain luxuries like food or gas for my car for the next two months, and bought the smaller, more expensive, but much brighter and better diamond for Ashley's ring.

This is what happens when we put our lives next to God.

We may think that we are doing some good things, but then we sit next to ultimate goodness and we realize that we aren't nearly as good as we first thought. We realize that there is something far brighter than we had imagined in the universe.

Far *holier*.

And this is the problem with having a holy God like this. When we think about him, even through the fog of humanity that keeps us from seeing him in all his brightness, we can't help but also think about how not-God we are. Darkness looks that much darker when it's next to something bright. Imperfection looks that much more imperfect when it's next to something perfect.

If you haven't had this kind of experience with God—this kind of awareness of who he is and who you are—then there really isn't a whole lot I can offer you right now in regard to prayer. This isn't the book for this kind of thing, but the short answer is you still have too much pride to admit to this kind of God that he is who he says he is—that he's *perfect*. And that you are who he says you are—*imperfect*. So you may want to skip the rest of this chapter and go do something else more useful on your spiritual journey. Like go look at the stars for a while and be reminded of how mysterious this life is. And how small you are.

But if you have had this kind of experience—where you become acutely aware of God's holiness and your lack of holiness, then there is some real hope for making progress in your relationship with him through prayer. Because you have the first and greatest thing needed to make this relationship sing—humility. You can—even if it's reluctantly—admit who God really is and who you really are. On one side of the relationship, there is perfection. On the other, imperfection.

With this awareness in place, we're ready to ask: How can a perfect God be a witness to an imperfect you and me? How can a relationship that is so mismatched continue?

There are two things to know at this point. And the first is far greater and more important than the second. The only way that we are able to be with God is because he is perfect. In an ironic sense, *his perfection makes it possible for our imperfection to be near him.* If we start with a God who is perfect, then we would also say that everything in him is perfect, as well. Or another way to say it is that everything that comes out of him would come out of him perfectly. For example, if God is loving, then he is *perfectly* loving. If God is patient, then he is *perfectly* patient. If God is kind, then he is *perfectly* kind. Or yet another way to say this is that this perfect God won't stop showing love, patience, kindness, or whatever else he wants to show to imperfect people because of their imperfection. In short, his ability to be perfect isn't based on our ability to be perfect, or even perfectly deserve his perfection. He remains independent of us, and unchanged.

When we understand this, we become free. Free from the anxiety that comes from having to perform. Free from the exhaustion that comes from having to pretend like we have it all together—whatever that means. Free from the self-righteousness and judgment that comes from applauding our good deeds, in an attempt to mask the self-pity and hatred that comes from our defeats.

And you know what happens when there is freedom in a relationship? When there is a strong assurance that we can show our true selves to someone and know that they will still accept us, love us, even like us and want to be with us?

Intimacy.

The more that we expose our imperfections and find safety and love on the other side of that exposure, the more we grow in our trust of that relationship. And the more we feel free to admit who we really are—brokenness and wounds and weaknesses and scars and all.

The holy God that the Bible talks about, that has changed billions of hearts, does exactly this. He accepts us just as we are, with no pretense. He loves us perfectly.

This is one of the most important aspects to grasp when we think about prayer. Once this awareness goes off in our hearts, once we know that the perfection next to us makes room for our imperfection, we know that we are safe. Because of his love, we can admit who we really are to him.

This is the second thing to understand about a relationship with a holy God. He does his part of loving us unconditionally. He then asks us to respond to this great gift of love with an accurate acknowledgment of who we are. This is called *repentance*. And it is one of the foundations of a powerful life of prayer.

Repentance gets a bad reputation in many circles, but the truth is there are few things more important to the spiritual life than this. In its simplest form, repentance is saying "I'm sorry" to a person whom you have offended or hurt. This simple form of repair fills even our earliest years. When we punch our brothers or say hurtful things to our friends or disrespect our parents, we learn to apologize as a form of mending the broken places of our relationships.

When God tells us to practice repentance, he most certainly means that we are to apologize to him (and to others, too). But he also means so much more than apology. Many of the words that we have in the Bible come to us loaded with images. For example, when we read that God possesses "glory," it doesn't just mean that he is "glorious" or having the traits and characteristics of someone who possesses this abstract idea of "glory." The word *glory* carries with it an image of something that can hold water without leaking, or weight without buckling. The idea here is that a glorious God is someone who is infinitely strong. He is trustworthy. So trustworthy, in fact, that he is like the Hoover Dam. And you can build your house at its base with confidence. Even though there is a massive amount of water raging above you, you're safe. He can hold it all. And he will never stop doing what he says he will do.

What a comfort this idea is. That God will never leak. He will never buckle. He will hold up when others weaken and fall.

The word *repentance* has its own picture. The idea behind this word is that an unrepentant person is someone who is walking in his own selfish direction. He does what he wants to do, says what he wants to say, lives how he wants to live without any regard for God. As he walks in his own direction, he hears a voice calling him. At first, he's not sure where this voice is coming from, but he eventually realizes that it's coming from behind him. "Come to me," it says. In order for this man to obey what he hears, he must first stop walking in his own direction, turn around, and walk in the other, opposite direction. With every step that he takes in this new, opposite direction, he moves farther away from his own original direction and closer to the voice that has called him. This is the image behind "repentance."

Every human heart, because of its self-centeredness, wants to walk its own way. And this way is *away* from God. We walk this way for a lot of reasons, but the consistent reason is because we are imperfect. Not holy. We think that we can live our lives without God and be happy, find fulfillment, and ease our sense of anxiety and loneliness.

When we repent, however, we admit that our way doesn't work. Our direction, no matter how seemingly innocent or good it appears, only moves us farther away from God. So much more than mere apology, repentance is an acknowledgment that we need to turn around. We need to abandon our self-centered and self-sufficient sense of direction. And we need to walk toward God.

In regard to prayer, the act of repentance has to be present in our spiritual rhythms. Often. Probably more often than we think. Because we are in the presence of an unchanging, perfect, *holy* God, one of the most important things we can do while we are in his presence is to admit who he really is. And by nature of that admission, another admission has to follow: we are not unchanging, we are not perfect, we are not *holy*.

In order to be in a relationship with this kind of a God, something has to cover this gap between his holiness and our selfishness. Christians believe that Jesus' sacrifice is this cover. But how do we appropriate that sacrifice into our hearts? Through repentance. Through admitting that we want to be happy and fulfilled and satisfied in the deepest parts of our souls, but we cannot reach any of these things through our own actions or self-generated direction. In fact, more than simply not being able to reach them, we *run the other way from them* through our selfishness and pride. Repentance—the act of saying that we are sorry combined with the act of turning away from our direction and walking in God's direction—lays down the road by which we experience relationship with him.

I've got one last thought about repenting in prayer. We don't need to make it too complicated. And we don't need to try to manufacture feelings of grief or sorrow around it, either. One of my favorite statements in the entire Bible is when the psalmist says, "God knows our frame, he remembers that we are dust" (Psalm 103:14). God knows who we really are. He has full knowledge of what kind of material he is working with when he walks with us. We don't need to pretend that we feel worse than we really do. And we certainly don't need to wallow. When we do something that goes in our own willful direction and against God's, we simply need to admit our wrongdoing and turn around. No emotions are required.

Certainly, if emotions are present, then great. We should thank God that he uses our emotions to get our attention. But emotions—even strong emotions like self-pity and guilt and shame—are not what get us back on the right road. Laying down our pride, admitting that we were wrong, and turning around are the kinds of things that move us in the direction we are supposed to go.

And this is the great freedom of dealing with a God like this, especially in prayer. We don't have to pretend to be something that we aren't. We don't have to warm our own hearts into an emotional state. All we have to do is admit that he knows what our lives need better than we do. Then we take a step in his direction, instead of our own.

And then we ask him to lead us.

12 FORGIVENESS

I WENT TO a strange college. My dad wanted me to go to the college that he attended, which was the same college that my mom attended, which was the same college that my older sister attended. I don't know a lot about birth order and the effects it has on someone's personality, but being the youngest kid in our family while at the same time being the first (and only) male kid, while at the same time being six years removed from my older sister, which meant that I grew up, in many ways, as an only child, meant that my dad had a zero-point-zero chance of seeing me go to his alma mater. I had to make my own way.

My own way was Oral Roberts University in Tulsa, Oklahoma. If you have never been to ORU, there is no possible way that I can explain it to you. But I will try. When you drive down to south Tulsa and turn onto Lewis Drive, the first thing you see is a pair of bronze hands pressed together in prayer. And they are massive. Like, Disney World massive. Surrounding these massive hands are dozens and dozens of flags from various nations. Not every nation, but most. I'd like to tell you that whoever picked these flags (and thereby excluded others) had a good reason for their selections. But that remains a mystery to me and everyone else who drives onto campus.

Things have changed now, but when I went there, ORU had other mysteries, as well. For example, male students had to be clean-shaven and wear a tie to every class, and have every breakfast and lunch in the dining hall. Pants were also a must—no shorts allowed because, apparently, kneecaps were just too scandalous. And don't even think about wearing open-toed shoes. Or letting your hair grow past your shirt collar. Female students had it the same, having to wear skirts or dresses to every class and have every breakfast and lunch in the dining hall. But they also had it worse, too. Every female student had to be back in her dorm by a curfew. I can't remember exactly what time it was, but all I remember is that we males didn't have a curfew. At all. Oral Roberts, the college's namesake, was known as a faith healer and a miracle-worker. The fact that this dual standard continued into the twenty-first century might be the greatest miracle of his entire career.

For all of its strangeness, my time at ORU gave me so many things that I wouldn't trade for all of the world. College is like that for many people—the best of times. But it was at ORU that I, in many ways, became a man.

One of the gifts that I experienced at ORU was an opportunity to lead an overseas mission team. Since I was a team leader, the Missions department had a strong interest in making sure that I didn't do something crazy like preach a heresy or lose money or date one of my teammates. So in an effort to address some of these potential pitfalls before we were an ocean away, the Missions department required every team leader to come to weekly trainings for several months leading up to our respective trips.

For the most part, these trainings covered fairly obvious stuff. I don't remember learning much during those meetings, but I do remember the friendships I made. And the prayers I prayed. When you're twenty-one years old and you aren't married and you have no kids and no mortgage and essentially no real responsibilities, it's almost amazing what you can get away with praying. And actually meaning. I honestly didn't care what God did with my life at that point. I just wanted to be useful to him. More than anything.

I also remember a camp that we had to go to as our final training before we left America and headed out to evangelize the world. It was about an hour or so away from campus. The seniors had already graduated and everyone else had already finished up their finals. Nearly all the students had gone home for the summer. For those of us who were traveling overseas, we had to spend a few days in some cabins in the woods to finalize the preparation for our trips and, more important, to cement a team-building process.

Which was filled with the usual stuff these kinds of team-building attempts include. Trust falls off picnic tables into your teammates' arms. Problem-solving exercises where we had to move rocks over streams with boards and twine. Sitting on upturned logs arranged in a circle while we shared our feelings with one another. Some people cried. We all laughed. Not at the people who were crying, but at something else. The usual.

One of the exercises we did as a group was a high ropes course. If you're not familiar with this type of thing, imagine a bunch of trees and telephone poles with ropes and cables strung up in them. High up in them, actually. You step into a harness, click into a belay system, and then try to make it through the suspended obstacles as a team. The idea is that some people will feel comfortable in this kind of setting and some won't. And a third group will pee themselves. The hope is that all three of these groups learn how to work together, despite their fears and frustrations, to accomplish a common goal—all while showing empathy and trust and patience and assertiveness and every other relational skill you would need if you were going to live in another country with a small group of people for the next month or two.

I don't love heights, but I didn't mind this exercise. For whatever reason, my feeling of responsibility for my teammates took over and whatever fear I had about hanging from a tree sixty feet in the air disappeared. It all felt easy.

Until the last obstacle.

After working through the other obstacles as a team, the final obstacle on the course was designed just for an individual. Once you zip-lined down from the last tree, you now stood at the base of a very tall and very in-the-middle-of-a-field-so-it-looks-even-taller telephone pole. I think I remember someone saying that it was eighty feet tall. But it might have been forty. The point is, it was T-A-L-L.

The goal of this obstacle was to teach you to let go. What that meant was that you had to make a solo climb up the telephone pole. Then, once you reached the top, you had to somehow find a way to get your feet on the top of the pole and stand up. Trust me. This sounds a lot easier than it actually is. Once you get to the last handle and footstep, there's nothing to reach for or hold on to for pulling up, steadying yourself on your feet, and then standing up. It requires a certain level of balance, strength, and fearlessness. Then, however, you're still not done. As you stand up on your perch, just past arm's reach, there is a trapeze bar floating in the thin air. Your job is now to jump into this thin air and hope that you can grab that bar. Because if you don't, you fall into nothing and pray that whoever is on your belay isn't picking her nose or checking his phone and actually pulls the slack out of the rope and keeps you from plummeting to the ground.

I wasn't the first one to make the attempt, but I was one of the first. I remember a few people getting up the pole, and a few more making the transition from climbing the pole to standing on top of the pole. But I don't remember anyone making the jump to the bar. Not because they weren't physically able to do it, but mainly because they would stop and look around once they had reached their perch and reality would set in about their current position in life. Once they started to think about how high they were, they lost the energy to focus on jumping for the bar. So by the time that they took a few deep breaths and tried to muster up that energy again, it was too late. Their legs couldn't find enough spring and they fell short.

Watching all of this, I decided that if I made it up the pole and if I made the transition to the perch on top of the pole, I was going to jump for the bar right away. No looking around and contemplating my death. Just climb up, stand up, and jump.

And that's exactly what I did.

I made it. People below me cheered, out of relief and surprise, I would bet. To see my gangly arms and legs involved in such an athletic feat had to shock them into some kind of reaction. I hung around on the bar for a few minutes, doing some pull-ups (back when I could still do pull-ups), and even pulled my legs through my arms and hung upside down for a few seconds. It wasn't because I was so proud or strong. It was because I was up there and I honestly didn't know what else to do. So I played.

This small victory didn't seem that profound when I originally experienced it. But looking back on it now, I see that climbing that telephone pole, lunging to the top of the perch, and then jumping out into nothing with a small hope that I might actually grasp something firm and steady is a lot like prayer. A specific kind of prayer, actually.

One of the most common experiences we have as relational beings is when someone wrongs us. It almost doesn't matter how severe the wronging is. They all hurt. Whether the wrong comes to us in the form of an older brother taking our favorite toy while we were playing with it or a spouse of thirty years having an affair with our best friend, we face the pain of people treating us poorly all the time.

How are we supposed to handle it when people wrong us? And what does prayer have to do with how we handle their wrongs?

We get some clues in the most famous prayer ever prayed: the Lord's Prayer. When some of Jesus' followers ask him about prayer, he gives them a relatively short way to pray. But within its shortness lies its genius. What it lacks in length, it possesses in simplicity and power.

> Our Father, who is in heaven.
> Hallowed be your name.

Your kingdom come, your will be done on earth as
it is in heaven.

Give us this day our daily bread.

Forgive us our debts, as we forgive our debtors.

Lead us not into temptation, but deliver us from
evil. (Matthew 6:9–13)

If I were the God of the universe and someone asked me
how to pray, I probably would be more inclined to give a different kind of answer. A *longer* kind of answer, mostly. But
here we have the best of starting points as to how we should
talk with God. And I'm grateful that in this succinct, almost
abbreviated model for prayer, Jesus acknowledges the fact that
we live within a world in which there exist real rights and real
wrongs. And I love that he goes even further and acknowledges
that these real wrongs come close to us, sometimes painfully
close, in the form of other people causing us pain.

Pain is not an easy thing to ignore. Sure, we can cover pain
up—both physical and emotional—with chemical substances.
But eventually it will return, alerting us that something isn't
right and demands our attention.

Anyone who has ever been in a relationship with anyone else
knows how true this is. When someone does something against
us, we feel pain. We might even feel violated. We might then
retreat to a comforting cave of alcohol or exercise or a glowing
screen or a pint of Häagen-Dazs, trying to find some sort of alle-
viation for our pain. But once the buzz wears off, once the endor-
phins die down, once the show is over, there we still are, hurt.
And we know that someone caused the hurt that we are feeling.

At this point, we have a few options. We can try to push this hurt aside and tell ourselves that it really doesn't matter that someone wronged us. This may work for a while, but eventually we will realize that no amount of pushing aside can take whatever pain we feel away. So maybe then we try something else. Maybe then we try to take revenge. We buy into the lie that the best answer for pain is more pain—even greater pain—and it will somehow make us feel better, feel more whole. Again, this might work for a season, but eventually we will realize that whatever pain we create in response to the pain we have suffered is nothing but a vase filled with dying flowers. What starts as something that we think will bring us life actually turns into death.

In his simple prayer, Jesus gives us a different way to face the wrongs of others. And he does it through a rich, powerful image. Imagine that you and I meet for lunch somewhere. I love Asian food, so let's say we meet at an Asian restaurant. We order. A lot. The food comes, which we enjoy, along with some nice conversation. The waiter drops off the check, at which point I tell you that I don't have my wallet with me and I need you to pay for my part of the bill.

If you're a kind person and especially if you enjoyed our time together, you might have no problem picking up the entire bill. You might even do it *joyfully*, as a gift to me. For which I would be grateful.

But now imagine something else. Imagine that when we first sat down for our lunch, I informed you that I didn't have my wallet. Internally you question why I even invited you to lunch and then so carelessly (intentionally?) forgot my wallet. You might even feel a bit offended. But in order to keep the peace and not ruin the meal, you graciously agree to pay for the entire lunch.

Let's keep imagining here. Imagine the same situation, only this time after you agree to pay for our lunch, the server comes to our table. He asks what we would like, to which you respond with a modest order. I, however, proceed to order far too much food. I order an appetizer, a salad, a cup of soup, and two entrées. And not just any entrées. The two most expensive entrées. At this point, you are almost certainly growing offended, and probably even resentful:

How dare he presume upon my kindness like this? He forgot his wallet and I am doing the gracious thing by paying for his meal. And how does he repay my graciousness? By ordering far too much food. And by ordering the most expensive food on the menu. What a…

You don't finish the sentence because you're trying not to swear.

But you want to.

Most of us would feel this way. We would feel taken advantage of. We would feel like something was being taken from us, instead of feeling like we were giving something freely.

Can I press this one level deeper?

This time, imagine that you are sitting at a table at this Asian restaurant by yourself. Suddenly I come and sit down at your table. We might know each other or we might not—that doesn't really matter for my point. The point is I sit down uninvited. And then I call the server over and start to order large amounts of the most expensive items on the menu. I even order the *duck*. Before the server leaves, I announce loudly: "This guy sitting across from me gets the check!"

At this point, most of us would move past offense and resentment and into sheer anger. Maybe even lividness. And we would probably begin to hate.

This is sort of what it feels like to be wronged. To be sinned against. When someone treats us as if his or her needs and wants are more important than ours (which is the essence of sin, unless it's God's needs and wants being more important than ours), we feel violated. Especially when we haven't invited them into our lives. We feel as if borders and boundaries have been unfairly crossed. We feel like something has been taken from us that we never intended to give.

Jesus knows these kinds of feelings. And it's why he identifies them in his instructions on prayer. When you come to God in prayer, I know that it's not just God and you that we have to talk about. We have to talk about God, you, and other people, too. Because you're not perfect and because everyone else isn't perfect, either, you are going to spend a large part of your life hurting others and being hurt by others. You won't be able to hide from this. And no amount of revenge will make the pain you cause or the pain you suffer go away.

Jesus tells us to pray in a way that lets all of this go. He tells us to pray in a way that shapes our hearts into givers of forgiveness.

When we violate God's will, we put ourselves into debt. And we trespass across a line. We violate something sacred. Because of that, we *owe*. And we put ourselves into places in which we don't belong, in which we don't have permission to be. We become the demanding person at lunch who presumes upon someone else's kindness, brashly taking something that isn't ours by right or by privilege. We put our needs and wants above God's.

This idea of a violation doesn't just apply to our relationship with God, either. It also applies to our relationships with others—and their relationships with us. When we hurt someone or when someone hurts us, an exchange happens. A *taking*. The person who has caused the hurtful exchange now owes a debt to the person he or she has hurt. Or another way to think about it is that a boundary line has been broken and someone has to make a repair. Like a broken-down fence or a kicked-in door, someone has to fix it.

So who pays the debt? Who fixes the fence?

This is another one of those things that is simple, but far from easy. Jesus tells us that the person who is offended, the person who is hurt, the person who is violated can pay the debt. He or she can fix the fence.

Forgive us our debts, as we forgive our debtors.

Notice that I didn't say *has* to. But *can*.

If you are the person who has been hurt, you can do whatever you want with that pain. Jesus doesn't stand over you in shame, forcing you into godliness. Pain hurts. Forgiveness is hard. But Jesus has something in mind when he asks us to forgive those who hurt us. Which is the same thing he has in mind when he forgives those who hurt him.

Freedom.

Anne Lamott has a wonderful way to illustrate this idea when she says, "Not forgiving is like drinking rat poison and then waiting for the rat to die."[1] That's exactly true. When we withhold forgiveness from someone, we think we are getting their attention by inflicting some sort of justice-inspired pain into their lives. But the exact opposite is true. In truth, we only injure ourselves. Because the person who has hurt us likely has gone on with his life, unconcerned or maybe even unaware of the pain that they have caused us. But we aren't unaware. And we aren't unconcerned. We still feel it, very deeply.

This pain often drives us to do something absurd. We think that by withholding mercy and grace and love and all the other things that go along with forgiveness—with settling a debt or fixing a fence—we are somehow tilting the world back onto an accurate scale of justice. *That will teach her to mess with me again. I'll just keep unforgiving her until she realizes how much pain she has caused. And then she'll pay.* But it's we who end up paying. When we withhold forgiveness from someone, we pay with unresolved anger. We pay with sleepless nights. We pay with our own bitterness. We pay with becoming a different, less-like-God person.

When we go to God in prayer, we usually hope to leave that time with two things. We hope to get him to do something (or give us something, like wisdom or peace) and we hope to be changed. In short, we want to rise from our time in prayer in a different world and as a different person than when we first began.

Forgiveness is vital to both of these experiences. When we choose to forgive someone, we create space for God to do something for us, mainly to forgive us. I can't say that I have this mystery completely figured out, but the Bible tells us two seemingly contradictory things. On the one hand, God tells us that our forgiveness depends solely on his unmerited love for us. It is unconditional, meaning that there is nothing that we can or can't do to either earn his forgiveness or nullify it. He is a forgiving God. It is in his character. And his character stands independent of our character (or lack thereof).

But the Bible also tells us that there is a connection between our willingness to forgive others and God's willingness to forgive us. There is no way of getting around it. This seems like a condition. If we forgive others, God will forgive us. If we withhold forgiveness from others, he will withhold forgiveness from us. (See Matthew 6:14–15.)

Somehow both of these things are simultaneously true. And I think it works a little like this. At the heart of forgiveness lies a surrender. We have to lay down our arms. We may be justly entitled to vengeance, or at least recompense, from someone who has hurt us. But that almost doesn't matter. Because we can't make someone apologize or give us restitution. Well, I guess we can in certain times (for example, you can make your kids apologize to you or you can manipulate your spouse through guilt or shame to apologize to you), but anyone who has done that knows it rings hollow when it comes and still leaves us wanting, long after it's over. It's like planning your own birthday party. What you want is to be celebrated by someone on his or her own accord. You want it to be their idea, so it feels sincere and not coerced.

So I think what God is getting at is when we are injured, we lay down our designs on justice and restitution. We choose to forgive the person who hurt us instead of hanging on to whatever is in our hearts we think we are entitled to. We—and this is the hard part—pay someone else's debt out of our own pocket. We fix the fence they so carelessly tore down.

All of this feels unfair—there's no way to get around

it—because *it is*. In a perfect world, you wouldn't have to pay someone else's debt. You wouldn't be responsible for fixing a fence that you didn't break. But as unfair as this is, it's actually a path to freedom.

Something happens when we lay down our arms and surrender. When we forgive someone, we essentially say, "God, I'm hurt. I want to take responsibility for this pain and make someone else hurt like I hurt. But instead of inflicting hurt and pain on this person, I know I need to let them off the hook. I need to pay their debt. I need to fix the fence. So I can be free from carrying around this burden of debt-paying, this burden of fence-fixing for the rest of my life."

And here is the connection between Jesus' seemingly contradictory words. The kind of person who can say something like this is the kind of person who understands mercy—to *not* give someone what they deserve. This is the kind of person who understands what God does for us through Jesus. He does not give us what we deserve and instead pays the debts we ring up and fixes the fences that we break because of our sins against him.

The two go hand-in-hand. If we truly understand that God forgives us—that he pays our debts and fixes our fences—then we will be the kind of people who are free to pay other people's debts and fix other people's fences. Because we know that we need the same thing that they need: *mercy*. Conversely, if we withhold forgiveness from other people, we essentially tell them, "Even though God treats me with mercy and doesn't give me what I deserve, I'm going to treat you differently and make sure that you get what you deserve." We do this all the time, and it makes no sense. It betrays the very heart of God.

So the call is to forgive. Everyone. Especially our enemies. Jesus did this when he was on the cross. He does this now, as he is seated next to his Father, as well. And he calls us to do the same. Because when we forgive others, we show our own hearts that we understand what it's like to be in need of someone else paying our debts, of fixing the fences that we have broken.

Back to the telephone pole story. When I stood on the top of the perch, ready to jump for the floating bar, I couldn't be two places at once. I couldn't remain in my position of relative security on the perch while at the same time enjoying the freedom of hanging from the bar. In short, I had to let go of something in order to experience something better.

This is why forgiveness is so important for our own hearts. While it may feel relatively safer and even better to hang on to a sense of justice, revenge, and unforgiveness, it isn't. There is a world of freedom on the other side of releasing someone into forgiveness. And God wants us to enjoy that world of freedom instead of carrying around burdens of justice and revenge that we were never meant to carry.

There are a lot of ways to do this. Maybe instead of nursing a wounded heart full of self-pity and resentment, we choose to show love and kindness to someone who has neglected us. Maybe instead of holding on to anger and violence toward someone who has injured us, we choose to turn them over to God and his justice (which is perfect, as compared to ours, which is not) and let it all go.

It has been my experience that forgiveness is less like an equation and more like an appetite. If you're looking for a way to balance the two sides of fairness or to calculate the exact amount of forgiveness needed for an offense, good luck. But if you see it more like an appetite that sometimes comes on strong and sometimes disappears into the background, then you are probably on the right track. Like all appetites, you can choose to starve it until it passes—which isn't a bad idea in certain times. For example, instead of eating that third dessert, you go to bed. Or you can choose to feed that appetite with something else. Something healthier. For example, instead of eating that third dessert, you reach for some almonds or a piece of fruit instead.

Both are good strategies for showing forgiveness to those who hurt you. And both are found in prayer. When we pray, we cut off the power of our appetite for revenge. *God, help me to forgive him. It feels nearly impossible, given what he's done to me. Which is why I need your help.* When we pray, we also feed our appetite for revenge with something else. *God, help me to see how much I need to be forgiven. I'm not perfect. I hurt people. I hurt you. And just like you show me love instead of justice, I'm asking for the power to show her love instead of justice, too.*

I cannot overemphasize how important all of this is. Undeserved forgiveness is at the center of any true relationship with God. So it would follow, it has to be at the center of any attempts at prayer we might make.

Which is why, when I'm praying in meaningful ways, my prayers almost always include the following two questions:

Where do I need to be forgiven?

Whom do I need to forgive?

Sometimes that's all I can get to in my prayers. But because of what I know about God, I know that it's a good start.

ONE OF THE great mysteries of this life is why God allowed the possibility of pain in the first place. I mean, why did he even create a world in which freedom and choice could lead to such destruction and devastation? Why not create a world in which nothing like the effects of sin could possibly come into existence? Sure, that would mean that human beings are limited in their ability to choose. But given the possibility of such severe consequences for our freedom—mainly, sin and death and all the things that we fight against in our lives—I would have no problem with a limited freedom if it meant that I could avoid all these things I hate, that cause me and so many others so much pain. Or in other words, don't give me a million dollars if by accepting that million dollars I also have to accept cancer and racism and murder and injustice and a lot of other cursed consequences. I would rather stay poor, and limited.

And yet here I am. Here *we* are. Living our lives in the unavoidable reality of pain. Every day.

If prayer doesn't help us process through the pain of our everyday lives, then what good is it? Either prayer helps us deal with the pain that we face in real and tangible ways or it is a hoax, completely useless and nothing more than a sanctified version of self-help and self-improvement.

When I'm hurting, I don't want prayer just to make me a better person. I don't want it just to settle me down and lower my blood pressure. I want it to *work*. Mainly, I want it to work something inside me that helps me go on, that helps me pick up the pieces and run toward the fight. I want something that gives me such an assurance on my insides that I can face anything. Especially pain.

How do we pray in this kind of way?

How do we pray in and through our pain?

Trying to picture God can sometimes—most times, actually—feel like a near impossibility. What does he look like? Is he big? Is he *really* big? Does he look kind? Or a bit judgmental? Does he look young? Or how about old? Is he lean and strong? Or soft and billowy like some sort of cosmic Santa Claus?

This last thought is where most of us land, if we're honest. We probably picture God as a mix of Santa Claus (the fat, jolly one), Abraham Lincoln (the one from the monument in Washington DC), and Charlton Heston as Moses ("Let my people go!"). He is a big, white-haired man who wears a beard while he sits on a large throne and stoically judges everyone. He has a booming, somewhat stern voice. He passes the time, somewhat boringly, giving good things to those whom he likes and bad things to those whom he doesn't. He doesn't like to be bothered, unless it's really important. And even then we can't be so sure.

This kind of picture of God reveals just how deeply we fail

to take the Bible—and the whole of Christian faith—seriously, and on its own terms. The Bible gives us an entirely different picture of God. Here are just a few images God uses to describe himself:

A friend who walks with us.

A fire that burns brightly in the night.

A cloud that shades as it leads in the day.

A still, small voice that whispers in the wind.

A mother hen who pulls her baby chicks up under her wing.

A tattoo artist who inscribes the names of those whom he loves on his hands.

A singer who loves to sing over his kids.

A loving father who runs toward his son, even though he has good reasons to withhold his love.

A dying son who promises compassion and grace to a criminal, hanging on a cross next to him.

A whimsical spirit who gives gifts to those who worship him.

A king who is so glorious that everyone bows in adoration to him.

These images are diverse for a reason. No single image can adequately portray the infinite complexity, beauty, and brilliance of God. Instead, each image offers us a road to greater understanding and appreciation of him. Different seasons in our lives require different roads. But they all lead to the same city. The city of God.

When we're in a season of pain, God gives us some specific roads to travel through prayer. And they come from the Psalms. Here is just a short list of how God tells us to think about him, especially when we are in trouble or are feeling pain:

A refuge
A strong tower
A shield
A firm foundation
A hiding place

The common denominator in each of these images comes across so clearly that it's almost too easy to miss. Each of these images should point us to this truth: God is somewhere that we can go when we are scared, when we feel sadness, when we face things that are much greater than we can handle in our strength. He is a refuge that provides us rest. He is a strong tower and a shield that provides us a defense. He is a firm foundation that never gives way. He is a hiding place that conceals us from the things that are trying to hurt us.

Each of these images should remind us about one aspect of God's character. Whatever else he is, he is someone who is *bigger than we are*. And he is someone who makes room for us, especially when we are on the run, so to speak. When we feel like something is chasing us—he is there, waiting for us to come to him. When we feel like something is hurting us—he is there, waiting to cover us with his love. When we feel like something is going to destroy us—he is there, waiting to defend us.

As objectively true as these things might be, that doesn't mean that our hearts live in the light of these truths. In fact, it's usually just the opposite. When we are afraid, when we feel pain, we feel like we are about to be destroyed, it's the darkness that usually wins in the arena of our souls. One of the effects of pain is not only the pain itself, but the haunting questions it brings with it.

What if this never gets better?

What if this gets worse?

What if my hopes and dreams never come to pass now?

What if this kills me?

In several seasons in my life, I have walked with these questions. Intimately. They have been (and sometimes still are) my faithful, horrible companions. They follow me everywhere and never seem to let up. Like Job's friends, they needle my heart in a way that leaves it raw, and afraid. And sometimes numb.

With these questions as my friends, I end up with more questions, as well. *God, are you there? God, are you good? Do you know what you're doing with my life? Why don't you act? Why don't you do something? Do you even hear me?* And finally, the most fatal of questions: *What's the point of trying to follow you anyway if you're not going to take away this pain that I'm feeling?*

These are big, deep questions. Questions like these have no easy answers. Many of them remain mysteries that we find ways to live with instead of resolutions to pronounce over. The real danger in questions like these, however, lies not in their unanswerable-ness. The real danger lies in what they do to our hearts.

Imagine a burning fire. I'm told that every fire needs three things to come into existence, and then to survive: fuel, oxygen, and a spark. Take away any of these three things and you don't have a fire anymore.

Now imagine your soul before a living, loving God. In Psalm 1, the author tells us that our souls are designed to be nourished by God, like trees planted by streams of living water. The living water is fresh and moving and contains within it a power to makes things grow in healthy, lush, strong ways. If you move the tree away from the water, or if the water somehow becomes polluted, or if the soil somehow grows dry, then the tree suffers. Eventually, it will no longer grow. And it will no longer be able to sustain its strength. Its leaves will fall. Its fruit will fail. And the tree will die.

This is the danger of what pain—especially unresolved pain—can do to our frail, dust-filled hearts. Our hearts were meant to burn toward God's direction. I don't mean literally burn, but I mean like the kind of burning you feel when you have your first crush, when your eyes first see a real ocean, when you come out of surgery and you realize that you're *alive*. There is supposed to be a fire in there. A warmth and a light that keep us mindful of God's goodness. And his nearness to us.

One of the things pain does is rob us of all of this. Pain assaults our understanding of God's character and causes the fire in our hearts to die. Like some sort of vacuum of the soul, pain sucks out all the oxygen from the room and the fire can't do anything but go out.

And then we become like the tree that is no longer planted

by the living water. Our leaves fall. Our fruit fails. Our roots dry up. And we die. Probably not literally, but certainly in a spiritual sense. Maybe we grow numb to the things of God. We don't care about reading the Bible. We don't have enough strength to lift our hearts in prayer. We don't even want to be around other followers of Jesus because, when we are, we feel only more isolated and alone.

Pain can keep us from God. There's no other way to say it. Why would we want to be with the person who is causing, or at least allowing, our pain to continue?

When our hearts get to this place, virtually nothing will help them. There is no amount of pleasure that we can experience that will make up for the brokenness we feel. No amount of alcohol or drugs or impulse purchases or chocolate or romance will take away our pain.

It is in these moments that we desperately need the very thing that we are trying to ignore. Like the man sitting on the tree, high above the ground, working his saw back and forth on the very branch upon which he sits, we have to somehow refuse the misplaced desire to cut off our connection with God. Because if we follow through on our desire to be free from him, we cut off the very thing that will give us the resources and the power to get through our pain. When we feel pain, we often succumb to the lie that we can somehow punish God by ignoring him. In truth, we punish only ourselves. And then without a branch to sit on, we fall. Often, very hard.

If we can somehow find the courage to pray in the midst of our pain, what happens? There are two things worth thinking about, maybe even clinging to. One we usually don't like at all, but the other is one of the most beautiful experiences of God's grace that anyone can have.

First things first. The one we won't like.

In many ways, we tend to go to prayer like Aladdin goes to his lamp. We need something. But we don't just need something—we need *something that we are unable to do using our own strength*. Emptied of our own efforts and out of ideas to solve our situation, we turn to prayer as a way to get what we can't give to ourselves. So we rub the lamp. We do this in different ways, but maybe we buy a new book with the hope of learning a new technique that will help us pray in more effective ways. Maybe we buy a new journal and a new pen and we commit to writing down our prayer requests, like some sort of writing-it-into-existence magic trick. Maybe we experiment with getting up earlier or staying up later or taking a walk or praying in the shower. The point is we try something new with an expectation of seeing our circumstances change. We think that God is in there somewhere and the reason why he isn't intervening in our situation is not because he doesn't want to or because he has a wiser, better reason for refraining, but because we just aren't doing the right things—praying the right way—in order to move him off his wire and into action on our behalf.

Let me be clear: none of these things are wrong. Sometimes we need to read a book about prayer to inspire us toward a fresh perspective or a new rhythm. And maybe we need to buy a new journal to help motivate us to take prayer more seriously. We might need to get up earlier.

The problem with this kind of approach to prayer is that it

betrays what we already know about God, as he has revealed himself to us through history, as recorded in the Bible. And here we get to the part that we're not going to like. At some point, we have to reckon with the hard, sometimes seemingly harsh truth that God has a much longer history of *not changing the circumstances around his followers than changing them*. No matter how hard we rub the lamp, sometimes things are going to stay the same.

Now, as soon as I type these words, I'm confronted with miracle after miracle in the Bible. The one with the Red Sea. The one with the fire from heaven and the fleeing prophets of Baal. The one where the woman who was infertile gets pregnant. The other one where the woman who was infertile gets pregnant. And the other one, too. The one where the guy is swallowed by a giant fish. The one where the leper gets his hand back. The one where the deaf man gets his hearing back. The one where the guy gets called back from a premature death.

The reality is there is a plethora of examples of God intervening in someone's story to save them or to heal them or to restore them. But there are just as many examples in the Bible—and the countless others that we don't have the privilege to read about—of God not answering the prayers of those who call out to him. Moses doesn't get to go into the Promised Land. David doesn't see his son live. Job doesn't get an explanation. Jeremiah doesn't find happiness. Jesus doesn't escape the cross.

A faith that doesn't make room—wide room—for these parts of the Bible is anemic at best, cruel at worst. Our God is a god who does whatever he wants to do. Sometimes that means he changes the circumstances around us. Other times it means that he doesn't. Regardless, and either way, we can be sure that whatever techniques we use or don't use to pray do not determine the outcome. That power is reserved for God alone.

When we pray, especially when we are facing pain, we have to come to our places of prayer with empty hands. There is a great prayer that Mother Teresa used to pray. It shows up in different forms in different places, and I can't find the direct quote (at least, accurately), but the idea is that she prayed:

> God, help me to take what you give and give what you take.

Now this is what empty hands look like on the ground of our daily lives, in prayer. In this short sentiment, we don't see someone who is trying to manipulate God into acting a certain way. We don't see someone who is anxious over her situations and asking God to change them, out of a place of anxiety. Instead we see a woman who has truly surrendered her life over to God, in trust. She has opened her hands. She has refused to rub the lamp. If God would change her circumstances, praise him. But if not, praise him all the same.

This is a hard place to get to, let alone live within. We naturally want to control things. Especially the things that give us pain. We don't have to understand the inner or outer dynamics around pain in order to try and make it end. Most of the pain we feel comes directly from our circumstances. The rest comes from them in indirect ways. In both instances, we want to somehow find freedom from whatever is hurting us. Which usually means that we want our circumstances to change.

When we pray, much of the fight is to resist this temptation to try to control our circumstances through our prayers. We also have to resist the temptation to try to control God into changing our circumstances. Again, this is very hard because pain is, in many ways, something that we can't control. One of the ways that we try to cope with things that we can't control is to—absurdly—double-down and try harder to control them. But God asks us to come to him with open hands. Hands that refuse to rub the lamp.

Once we refuse to try to control God—even if it's only in part—we help make room for something else to happen. Something far more productive than any attempt at control we could ever make. And this is the part of praying through our pain that we desperately need.

In one of Paul's letters to a church in Corinth, he addresses his usual concerns. He wants his readers to love each other better and to stop acting so crazy. He wants the church to be faithful to his teachings, specifically in the area of money and generosity. He wants people to know about Jesus. But then toward the end, he gives them (and us) a glimpse into his reality—a reality which included a lot of pain.

Picture one of the greatest leaders of the Christian faith, one of the strongest minds and most devoted hearts of our Christian history, writing these words:

Five times I received at the hands of the Jews the forty lashes less one. Three times I was beaten with rods. Once I was stoned. Three times I was shipwrecked; a night and a day I was adrift at sea; on frequent journeys, in danger from rivers, danger from robbers, danger from my own people, danger from Gentiles, danger in the city, danger in the wilderness, danger at sea, danger from false brothers; in toil and hardship, through many a sleepless night, in hunger and thirst, often without food, in cold and exposure. And, apart from other things, there is the daily pressure on me of anxiety for all the churches. (2 Corinthians 11:24–29)

This almost seems made up. Beaten to near-death not once, but five times. Stoned. With real rocks. Shipwrecked. Constantly on the run. Hungry. Sleepless. And "other things" that we can only imagine had all made life incredibly difficult for Paul. Then, on top of all of his personal sufferings, he had to bear with the churches that he had started and all of their sufferings, too.

It doesn't seem fair. In truth, it *wasn't* fair. A great man like Paul shouldn't have had to endure such pain. He should have been camped out in a nice house somewhere on the Mediterranean with a few servants, some olives, and a nice multibook deal with the biggest publisher of the day. And yet here he is, listing off just a part of his pain-filled story.

If anyone had been tempted to expect God to change his circumstances, it would have been someone who'd gone through these kinds of events. I can almost hear Paul now:

"God, what are you doing with my life? I've given everything to you. And this is how you repay me? It's not fair. It's not right. I deserve better. You need to change these horrible circumstances. NOW."

Maybe Paul prayed prayers like this. Part of me hopes that

he did, so I could then comfort myself with the fact that I'm not the only one praying these kinds of prayers when I face my pain. But Paul gives us a different, far more comforting type of prayer than mere complaints:

> I know a man in Christ who fourteen years ago was caught up to the third heaven—whether in the body or out of the body I do not know, God knows. And I know that this man was caught up into paradise—whether in the body or out of the body I do not know, God knows—and he heard things that cannot be told, which man may not utter. On behalf of this man I will boast, but on my own behalf I will not boast, except of my weaknesses—though if I should wish to boast, I would not be a fool, for I would be speaking the truth; but I refrain from it, so that no one may think more of me than he sees in me or hears from me. So to keep me from becoming conceited because of the surpassing greatness of the revelations, a thorn was given me in the flesh, a messenger of Satan to harass me, to keep me from becoming conceited. Three times I pleaded with the Lord about this, that it should leave me. But he said to me, "My grace is sufficient for you, for my power is made perfect in weakness." Therefore I will boast all the more gladly of my weaknesses, so that the power of Christ may rest upon me. For the sake of Christ, then, I am content with weaknesses, insults, hardships, persecutions, and calamities. For when I am weak, then I am strong. (2 Corinthians 12:2–10)

Paul is subversively talking about himself here—he is the "man in Christ." One of the things that Paul isn't subversive about, however, is the weakness and brokenness he experienced. Theologians and biblical scholars and pretty much anyone who has ever read this passage have all wondered what was causing Paul's weakness and brokenness. He doesn't share it directly here—and there are a lot of good reasons why it all remains a mystery—but what he does share is that it felt like a thorn.

The image of a thorn has strong biblical precedents—one of which is worth briefly mentioning. In the very beginning of Creation when Adam and Eve disobey God's command and eat the forbidden fruit, one of the consequences of their disobedience was that work—especially for Adam and, consequently, every man since—would produce *thorns*. Metaphorically this means that Creation has gone astray. Before sin entered into the world, work would have produced fruit and fruit alone. God first set up our relationship with the world to operate under this idea of sowing and reaping. Meaning, when one of his kids sowed work into Creation, he or she would reap fruit—or, that is to say, something good. But now, because of sin, this wouldn't always be the case. Now, because of sin, even our best attempts at sowing good things would sometimes give us something painful and broken—thorns.

This is what Paul is talking about here. He was engaged in work—holy work, even. And where he expected to find fruit, he instead found a thorn. Or maybe even *thorns*—plural. Like most of us would do, he went to God and asked him to deal with these thorns. Mainly, to change his circumstances. God, however, refused. We, of course, don't know all the reasons why God made this refusal, but we can at least know that God wasn't doing anything new here. There was another man who was dealing with different kinds of thorns, as well, and when he asked God to take them away, God refused to do so. Instead, God allowed him to face these thorns in a very personal, painful way. Namely, he allowed them to be shaped into a crown and pressed into his skull.

But back to Paul. What we see here is something so beautiful that it can only come from God. In the midst of his pain, Paul pours out his hurting heart to God, begging him (three times!) to take the pain away. Instead of taking it away, God gives Paul something better. He gives him an assurance:

> "My grace is sufficient for you, for my power is made perfect in weakness."

God tells Paul that something about his pain and weakness and brokenness is a vehicle for a deeper, much greater experience of his grace.

At this point, we have to admit that we don't know much about this kind of prayer. Most of us will try to do whatever we can to minimize pain and discomfort in our lives. Out of these desires, we will turn to God in panicked worry, asking God to remove whatever pain we are experiencing.

But we simply can't pass over this foundational truth God shows us here. He will not be hurried. He will not be moved. He never promises to remove our pain, at least not in this lifetime. And he has his reasons. But he will also never ask us to walk through pain without also promising to give us an assurance of grace. He is sufficient. He put his power in our weakest places. He makes us strong in the midst of our brokenness. Because he loves us.

When we're hurting, it is tempting to think that what we really need is an absence of pain. I get that. Very much so, actually. I don't want pain in my life, either. But this powerful exchange between God and Paul reminds me—even if I don't like it—that God wants something greater for me and my life, for me and my soul, than an absence of pain. He wants a presence of grace. A presence of his love. Of his strength.

As backward as this sounds, this is actually a really good thing that God works like this. If I bring to him my weakness and brokenness and pain and then he immediately takes it away, I run the risk of remaining a spiritually shallow person. I wouldn't know what it means to lean on God and cling to him as a drowning man clings to a life preserver. And I wouldn't know what it means to experience God's love, independent of my circumstances. Too often I can equate a good and pain-free life with God's blessing. Conversely, I can equate a hard and pain-filled life with God's cursing. Which means that my job as a Christian is to live a good enough life to maximize God's blessings and limit his curses. If things go wrong and my life turns out to be hard—maybe even *really* hard—then I can only slip into a place of self-blame and anxiety. *Maybe I'm not living a good enough life to deserve God's grace right now.*

And here is the beauty in Paul's experience. By not agreeing to remove the thorn, God is saving Paul's soul. He is making war against a belief that a well-lived life equals a pain-free life. He is reminding Paul that the presence of pain in his life is not an indication of God's absence. The presence of pain actually makes room for God's presence.

Let me be clear: this is the assurance that every single person who has ever lived needs. Suffering is the greatest mystery of this life. Why do bad things happen to us? No one has a definitive answer. No one. But what Christianity gives us is something better than an answer. God gives us an assurance that he will work within whatever bad things that happen to us. He will fill our weakness with his strength. So that we can say, "When I am weak, then I am strong."

This kind of assurance comes strongest through prayer. If we can somehow let our pain drive us to God instead of away from him, and if we can resist the urge to treat God like some sort of cosmic genie whom we expect to change our circumstances, we have a better than good shot at experiencing it. And like Paul, being able to say, "I am not strong enough to keep facing this kind of pain on my own. But I am not on my own. I have access to a God who promises to be with me when who I am is not enough."

And isn't this one of the great desires behind every prayer we pray? To know that it's truly okay to admit our limitations, and then to know that God is still there, sitting next to us, loving us?

In many ways, our hearts are too small. They are too small for life and God and all the beauty that both of these two things possess. One of the ways that our hearts grow is through pain. It's through pain that we learn to appreciate relief. To take notice of it. It's through darkness that we learn to be aware of the light. It's through our own frailties and sufferings that we learn the true meaning of God's assuring sufficiency and love.

Let me point to just one story that shows just how true this is. Paul Tillich was a German theologian who lived in the twentieth century. When he was recounting his life in his memoir, he noted that he had trouble appreciating art and beauty when he was a younger man, even going so far as to say that it left him "cold." But then something happened: World War I. Tillich was selected to serve in the fight and saw three quarters of his battalion die in battle. He saw, maybe for the first time in his life, real pain. Real suffering. And it changed him. While on leave from the war effort, Tillich found himself in a small corner of a museum in Berlin, staring at a painting of Mary and Jesus and some angels singing. Normally, this scene would have left him unmoved. But because of the pain and sorrow he had just endured, he now wept. Loudly. Deeply. He was moved by the beauty before him because it represented to him freedom from the pain that lived behind him.

Commenting on this story, author and philosopher Alain de Botton says, "It is in dialogue with pain that many beautiful things acquire their value."[1] This is exactly right. Our lives are like ongoing conversations. Sometimes we hear good and noble things spoken to us. Other times, we hear evil and painful things spoken to us. Part of what it means to make peace with life and God is to recognize these twin realities and then to keep them in dialogue with each other.

When we experience goodness and beauty, we celebrate and laugh and let out tears and cries of happiness and joy. When we experience pain and suffering, we mourn and feel sad and let out tears and cries of sorrow and frustration. Both of these experiences can bring us to a place of beauty. There is a beauty that exists only in the setting sun over the infinite horizon of a royal blue ocean. But there is also a beauty that exists only in the broken heart that refuses to quit crying out to God, asking him for help.

As much as we might want to fight against it, pain can lead us to beauty. And it can help us learn how to pray. If only we would let it.

I've had too many of these experiences to write about here. But one particular season is worth mentioning. After serving as a pastor for several years, I wasn't sure I wanted to continue in this profession. I was tired and lonely. I had entered into pastoral ministry with some false hopes. And the process of shattering those hopes was proving to be painful.

It was during this season that I sensed God calling me to prayer. Late at night, after everyone had gone to sleep and I was alone in a quiet and dark house, I would head out to the living room, read a little bit of the Bible, and try to pray. I prayed that God would take away my feelings of despair. I asked him to send something new, something different, into my life to ease my weakness. I tried to hope. I tried to make sense out of my life and God's workings within it.

This went on for months. And in many respects, nothing really happened during these times of prayer. I wish I could say that I emerged from those late-night attempts to find God with a greater confidence in him, with a stronger hope in him. But quite honestly, I often felt the same pain in the morning that I had felt the day before.

It wasn't until years later I realized, partially, what God was doing in that season. He was teaching me how to use my pain.

Just like a sore knee drives us to the doctor for an MRI to see what's going on inside of it, pain can drive us to God to see what's going on inside of us.

And this is a beautiful thing.

Because when we are in pain, God is the one we really need.

So maybe we pray things like this:

God, I'm hurting. I have some ideas about why I'm hurting, how things could be better, how my life should go. But I'm not the doctor here. You are. All I know is that I'm in pain. And I'm coming to you because you say that you can enter into what's really going on in my heart and give me things like comfort, peace, hope, strength, relief. These are things that I need. Help me to surrender to you. To yield to you. To trust you.

This—or some version of this—is one of the most meaningful prayers we can pray. Because it not only acknowledges our pain, but it acknowledges God, as well. And our souls need both.

I REALIZE THAT, up to this point, I haven't been very practical. What I mean is that I know that if I were going to spend some of my valuable time reading a book about prayer, one of the main things I would want to see happen as a return on my investment is that I would come away with a new system, a new way of organizing my prayer life so that it would *run better*.

I have intentionally resisted my own urges here. In many ways, nothing would be easier than to write a book based around some key principles that I have either seen work in my life or that I have heard work in someone else's life. I could identify these principles, surround them with some witty stories that are vulnerable, but not *too* vulnerable, add a few quotations from some respected thinkers, and be done.

If I'm being honest, I love those kinds of books. For two reasons. The first reason is that I can read them quickly. The second reason is that I feel like those types of books make their respective subjects manageable. Like I will be able to relatively easily implement the techniques they recommend into my life and then somehow my life will become different.

The problem with both of these reasons—for me, at least—is that they expose the two places of my heart that need the most work. Speed does not often lead me to depth. Very rarely do we become the kinds of people that God wants us to become if we value immediacy over patience and, to go even further, *long-suffering*. Character takes time to forge, to grow. The very act of breezing through a book too quickly misses the point. Yes—I checked something off my list. And for a brief moment, I carry around an empowering sense of accomplishment. But that sense fades, sometimes within the same day, the same hour. And my character—who I *am*—remains unchanged. I'm not trying to make a comment on the character or even intentions of any author out there. I'm just saying that a book that reduces something as mysterious and beautiful and complicated and *slow* as spiritual growth into mere principles or sound bites leaves me at the very best hollow and at the very worst suspicious. I like ingesting these kinds of books the same way I like ingesting ice cream. They taste good on the tongue. And they taste good going down. But they leave me without the satisfaction of real nourishment.

The other problem with reducing something like our spiritual growth down to techniques is that they are quite often not replicable. Take this issue of prayer. I have read books written by godly men and women who recommend—strongly—to start every day with prayer. Which means that you have to get up early in the morning. And they might have a point. In fact, there are even some great passages of the Bible that assure me they do. But I have also read books by other godly men and women who—thankfully—had the courage to confess their struggle to pray in the early morning hours. Instead, these pilgrims found that they could best pray at other times during their day.

The same goes for the amount of time spent in prayer. Some authors would say that we should carve out long periods of time for prayer. Others would say that we best experience prayer through short, frequent looks to God rather than longer sessions.

Who is to say who is right?

Certainly not me. But what I can say is that all the relationships in my life that mean something bear no resemblance to a system based on my ability to perform certain rhythms or techniques over and over again. I most often experience intimacy with my family and friends through my flexibility. Sometimes my wife wants to talk with me about her feelings. Sometimes she wants to watch a movie. Alone, even. Sometimes my kids want me to ask them about the details of their days. Sometimes they want me to chase them around the living room and tickle them until they cry.

Relationships—true, intimate, satisfying relationships—run best on our ability to be present with the other person. Not on our ability to always say the right things, perform the right ways, or master the right techniques.

Our relationship with God is no different. He doesn't ask us to develop a system for talking to him. What he wants is for us simply to be present with him. Speaking. Listening. Responding. Letting him respond. All the (slow) while, building intimacy, or with-ness, with each other.

But, of course, I get stuck.

And everything I just wrote slips through the fingers of my soul like water. I forget that God doesn't care that much about how I say things to him. Or even when. So I try all the practical tricks I've heard in sermons or read in books.

I set my alarm and get up before the sun and try to pray.

I buy a new journal, hoping it will inspire me to keep a prayer list.

I try to be still.

When that doesn't work, I try taking walks.

I try to pray the ACTS way that I've heard about from so many people since I was young. A: "adoration." So I try to adore God. C: "confession." I confess all the sins that I can think of to him, even the ones I've confessed before. T: "thanksgiving." I thank God for everything I can think of, too. S: "supplication." I ask him for stuff.

When that doesn't work, I pick up a collection of prayers written by some Puritans.

When that doesn't work, I read a book by C. S. Lewis.

Sometimes I stay up late, after the rest of my family has gone to bed, and I pray alone, in the dark of night. I bow down and press my face against the ground. I lean over my knees and put my face in my hands.

Sometimes I turn on music.

Sometimes I turn off every sound I can find.

I pray silently.

I pray out loud.

I pray in solitude.

I pray with other people.

In short, I take every practical step I know to take to try

and find God. Some of these steps will work, for a while. But eventually they all grow cold, or I should say that I grow cold to them. And I feel stuck.

So what do I do *then*?

Instead of running to a set of practical tips or a recommended system of engagement with God, I find that one of the best ways to move past the struggle of being stuck in my prayers is to look at one of the most famous—if not *the* most famous—prayers in the entire Christian tradition: the Lord's Prayer. I briefly wrote about one aspect of this prayer in chapter 12, but now I want to go a bit further with it.

I'm not doing anything novel here. Apparently prayer has always felt hard and confusing and mysterious yet compelling all at the same time because one of the men who followed Jesus around and became convinced that he had the answers for his heart and life came to him one time and almost sheepishly asked him, "Lord, teach us to pray, as John taught his disciples."

Most people jump straight to how Jesus answers, which is such a famous answer that I might not need to quote it again, but here goes:

> Our Father, who is in heaven,
> hallowed be your name.
> Your kingdom come, your will be done on earth as
> it is in heaven.
> Give us today our daily bread,
> and forgive us our debts, as we forgive our debtors.

Lead us not into temptation, but deliver us from evil. (Matthew 6:9–13)

These few words are as rich and beautiful as they are true. But they are often misunderstood. Because of our heart's desire to perform, and its subsequent desire to know that it has done enough to get off the hook of punishment, and because of its *other* subsequent desire to be free from the guilt that arises when it doesn't perform well enough, we usually take these few lines and start to craft a system out of them. We then try to work these principles into our hearts by reciting these words almost like an incantation. We pray these same words over and over again, but never truly reflect on what they mean and, more important, *how* they mean it. And even more important than that, *what kind of life Jesus envisioned when he gave us these words.*

We shouldn't feel too badly about this. The disciple who asked Jesus how to pray had similar things in mind. He had heard that John—another religious leader at the time—was off in the corner of his own world, eating locusts and honey, wearing burlap, and at the same time had stumbled onto something with the God of the universe. Whether this next part is true or not doesn't really matter, but the perception going around about John was that he was a deeply spiritual man who was able to pass on some of this spirituality to his followers by teaching them certain, specific ways to pray.

This shouldn't escape us. This is nearly identical to how most Christians I know approach prayer, as well. We come into contact with someone who we think is godly and spiritually proficient in things like prayer and the first thing we ask him or her is, "Okay, so how do you do what you do? Clue me in on the secret so I can be the same way that you are."

This isn't a bad question—far from it. Most of us grow best when we have examples to follow. But notice what Jesus does here. He could have answered the request in much clearer ways. For example, he could have said something about exactly when he prays. Or how he sits (or stands) when he prays. He could have recited a profound or memorable passage from the Old Testament. He could have stressed the importance of silence. He could have created an on-the-spot acronym that held the keys to intimacy with God.

And yet he did none of these things.

In fact, this is one of those parts of the Bible where I read it and I almost immediately say, "That can't be the whole story. What *else* did he say?"

The Lord's Prayer amazes me not only for what is in it, but also almost as much for what is *not* in it. And whatever we might think about this famous prayer, we have to at least say that it could have been a lot longer. If I were the Son of God and someone asked me how to talk with him, I would have a lot more to say than these few things about God being our Father, him having a plan for how the world should go, some bread, some forgiveness, and some evil.

Perhaps Jesus was interrupted. Or perhaps he knew that these few lines contained all that we need to know about developing a simple trust in God as our Father. I don't know why it's so short, but I do know that these few thoughts have become so famous for a reason. And the reason isn't because they give us a system or a technique.

These few lines give us so much more than a spiritual checklist to work through before we move on to pray about other things. In truth, there aren't "other things" that lie outside this prayer's reach. Consider what Jesus is really telling us here.

Our Father...

Whatever I think about God, he is, first and foremost, a Father. If God is my Father, how did I get into his family, being so broken and weak and sinful as I am? Well, now I have to think about adoption. I have to think about how God set his love upon me and invited me in. I have to think about how he made a way for me through Jesus to be in a familial relationship with him. And I have to think about how he now treats me as his firstborn son, just like he treats Jesus. Which means, at the very least, that he loves me and I can trust him.

...who is in heaven...

This God who invited me into his family has his eyes on other things besides this earthly world. His perspective is different from mine. He sees the whole picture, while I see only a part of it. Now I have to think about just how *ultimately qualified* this God is to hear me, and to handle whatever I bring to him with wisdom, righteousness, and justice. He sees all. He is over all.

... hallowed be your name...

Hallowed isn't a word we use very often today, but it simply means "holy." *Holy* is a significant word in the Bible and is used to show that something is special, or set apart for a special purpose. Here it helps to have a little knowledge of the biblical world. In ancient times, a name was more than just a name. A name carried with it a sense of authority, character, and power in direct relationship to its owner. That is why we see God changing people's names so often. When he gave someone a new name, it was a sign to the rest of the world that a new authority, character, and power was now in operation in this someone's life. So when I come to this part of the prayer, I have to think about how God's authority, character, and power are special. In fact, the God that I'm dealing with through prayer is so special that even his name reflects just how special he is. In short, there is no other "God." He alone can carry that name, and all that comes with it.

... your kingdom come, your will be done on earth as it is in heaven...

Here we have the second main image we need to have when we think about God. As the prayer begins, we see God as a *Father*. Now, as we get rolling a bit, we see him as a *King*.

This is what's implied when Jesus tells us that God has a King-dom. Who has kingdoms? Only kings. So as much as I want to see God as a kind and tender Father who loves me—which is true—I also have to accept the truth that this same kind and tender Father is also a sovereign and powerful King. He is both on the throne and on the move, so to speak. He governs over everything. But he also commands a cosmic renewal effort that begins in heaven, from his throne, and is steadily advancing throughout the earth, our home. Part of what it means for me to pray to this Father-King God is that I recognize this renewal effort and I ask to be a part of it.

...give us this day our daily bread...

But life isn't just about such lofty, spiritual things. Yes—God is on the move and is building out his spiritual Kingdom on and in our earthly home. But I also live in this very physical body. And this body has needs, like food and water and shel-ter and rest. Again, it is helpful to understand a little about the ancient world here. Bread was seen as the most common, most basic form of nutrition. In a very real sense, bread was the foun-dation of everyone's culinary experience. So when Jesus tells me to ask God for bread, he is telling me to ask God to provide for and sustain my most basic of needs. This doesn't mean that I can't ask God for things that go beyond my most basic of needs. Rather, this means that I need to spend some time remembering how God is the provider and sustainer of my entire life. Every-thing. My breath. My blood. My bones. My bread.

...and forgive us our debts...

It's not too far of a jump to get to a place of confession from here. So much of my life, I fail to see God as a loving Father. I fail to honor him as the true King. I fail to live in a way that makes his Kingdom possible around me. I fail to remember with gratitude how God provides for me at the most basic of levels. And a whole host of other things I have done and continue to do wrong come up at this point, as well. So I ask God to forgive me. I can't save myself. I can't pay off my own debts. I can't fix my own broken fences. I need God to do all of this for me. He is my only hope.

...as we also have forgiven our debtors...

God's love and care and provision for our lives come with a plan. He plans to press his love so deeply into our hearts that it starts to leak out toward others. One of the very practical ways this works is with this issue of forgiveness. If God forgives me for all of my shortcomings and wrongdoings—which he does—then who am I to withhold forgiveness from someone? The humbling truth that I need to be forgiven should push me to a place of extending forgiveness to those who have hurt or mistreated me. There's no way around this. Truly forgiven people forgive people. Because they are acutely aware of their own need for mercy, they are able to graciously and generously give mercy to others. The Lord's Prayer puts this reciprocal activity front and center and does not let me escape. When I'm dealing with God, he asks me to consider how I'm dealing with the rest of his kids. Even the ones who sin against me. Especially those, actually.

...And lead us not into temptation...

Out of the frying pan and into the fire. Let's say that we enter into a time of prayer and confess our sins to God. We also confront just how unforgiving we are of others, so we end up confessing that, too. After a period of time, we emerge from our time of prayer with a clear assurance of our own forgiveness as well as a relatively strong assurance that we have forgiven all the people who have sinned against us. Now what? Maybe it's an hour later, or even a day later, or maybe it's just a few minutes later and those clear senses of assurance are gone. They have disappeared. We forget about God's mercy and kindness. We forget about his love for us. And instead we find ourselves now facing urges to do really unspiritual, ungodly things. The great thing about this prayer is it reminds me that this is normal. Temptation to both avoid God and disobey him is all around me. It's part of the reality that I have to face as long as I live in this world. To think otherwise is to live in ignorance. So I pray that God keeps my heart soft toward him and hard toward the things that lead me away from him.

...but deliver us from evil...

The story about a man or a woman or even a nation held in captivity, but then finding freedom from that captivity because of God's redeeming love, is one of the main narratives of the Bible. In fact, this is one of the main images that the writers of the New Testament use to describe what the Christian life actually looks like. There is evil all around us. And even more specifically, there is an evil adversary all around us, too. Because of Jesus, this evil is defeated. But because of God's patience, it has not been totally eradicated yet. Jesus tells us that God is allowing evil to continue to grow along with the good in this world as a way of giving all of us more time to turn to him in repentance and gratitude. One day, God will end his time of patience and come as the warrior that he is, eradicating evil once and for all. Until then, however, I have to remember to ask him to deliver me from all the places that evil touches in my life.

See how different all of this is from mere technique? Jesus gives us more than a blueprint for "mastering" prayer. He gives us the language of our hearts. Everything I face in my daily life, every desire I have for freedom and goodness, every fear I have about the future—Jesus addresses them all in these few lines. All of them.

The Lord's Prayer isn't a list of exercises through which we have to work. It isn't a rulebook for how to pray or not to pray. There isn't some mystical or magical power hidden within it that can come out only if we recite it over and over again.

The Lord's Prayer is like scaffolding for a painting on a very tall wall. It has to be erected before any work can be done. And that's what it does, for me at least. When I slow down and focus on these few lines, I find that Jesus' words of instruction build up the values that I need to think about when I'm praying. These words remind me that I need to trust God because he's the Father. They remind me that whatever is happening in my life can be used to further the True King's Kingdom. They remind me that everything that I have in my life came from God, and he will sustain me as long as he sees fit. They remind me to be humble, and to ask for forgiveness. They remind me to be the kind of person who is merciful, and to extend forgiveness to others. They remind me that, even though I can't see it, there is a spiritual reality to my existence. And that spiritual reality isn't always full of good things. So I need to ask God to protect me and keep me from the evil forces behind the scenes of my life.

These are things that I truly need.

One more place of honesty here.

Even all of this can grow cold, too.

No matter how hard I try to remember these things when I read and pray the Lord's Prayer, it can become something of a rote exercise. I feel like I'm just saying words. Like singing the National Anthem at a baseball game. I know the words are supposed to signify something that speaks to a greater truth. But my mind wanders and I feel far from whatever truth I'm supposed to be thinking about.

It's in these lean times that I try to come back to a little exercise I stumbled upon a few years ago. In an effort to warm my heart to the things God talks about in this prayer, I go off-script a bit and I try to pray the Lord's Prayer in my own words. This isn't because I think the words found in the Bible are insufficient or somehow lacking in punch or power. Rather, it's my own attempt to awaken my heart to what it should be thinking, feeling, and asking while praying this prayer.

It changes a bit, depending on what's in my heart at the time, but here is generally what I end up praying when I do this:

God, thank you for being a good and loving Father. You love me and make room for me in your family. I'm grateful to be in your family.

Thank you that you're in heaven. You are so special that you get your own place. You are high above me and see everything in my life.

You're so special that even your name is special, God. Help me to think about that when I say your name in this prayer.

God, I want the way that you do things in heaven to be the way that I do things on earth. Thank you for being the True King.

God, I'm asking for you to provide for me. Thank you for providing for me today. Help me to trust you to provide for me tomorrow.

Forgive me for where I haven't done what you wanted me to do.

And help me to be the kind of person who forgives others, when they haven't done what I wanted them to do.

Keep me from anything that is not of you, God. Protect me from evil. Help me to live a life that honors you in all that I do.

I love you, God. Thank you for hearing me because of Jesus. It's in his character, power, and authority that I pray these things.

Amen.

That's basically it. I don't do this every day, or even every week. But when I get stuck and my heart seems cold to the things of God, this kind of prayer is my home. It's my North. It's where I start from. And then I ask for everything else to follow.

Which is what I think Jesus was getting at when he answered his disciple. We know that Jesus prayed in a lot of different ways. Sometimes he stood. Sometimes he kneeled. Sometimes he was with others. Sometimes he was alone. Sometimes he prayed in the morning. Sometimes he prayed late into the night. The point is, our prayer rhythms are supposed to be rich and fluid. They are supposed to travel with us throughout our daily lives, in all of their complexity and fullness. But we have to start from somewhere. And this kind of prayer—the Lord's Prayer—is where Jesus tells us to begin.

THE GREAT HOPE of prayer is not that things would change, but that we would be changed. Which is easier said than done. Change, just like prayer, is often hard. But it is possible.

Sometimes we change because something inside us switches. For various reasons, our hearts move from one place to another and we find ourselves seeing the world, others, ourselves, and God differently. Then, our actions follow. Take, for example, the lifelong smoker who hears the doctor say that he sees a spot on her lung. An inner reality shifts, which then leads to different actions and practices. The woman leaves the doctor's office, explores some options on how to quit smoking, then decides to quit—or at least try to quit. Her actions changed because of an inner desire to live differently.

But change doesn't always work like this. Sometimes our hearts are so wayward, so inherently committed to their positions, that they need to be remolded. They need to be trained in new desires, new ways of seeing the world. How does this happen? This is the other way in which we change. We start with new practices or actions that eventually, when done long enough and devoutly enough, cut new channels of growth into our hearts and leave us thinking and believing differently. For example, think about someone who is addicted to sugar. He loves sugar. And yet he knows that eating sugar to excess is unhealthy for him. So against every desire within him, he decides to quit cold-turkey. He audits his pantry and throws away his stash of comfort food. When he eats out at a restaurant, he skips dessert. He eats nuts. Or worse, kale. In short, he implements new behaviors in his life, even though his heart doesn't desire them.

Then, after several weeks of doing this, he finds something surprising has happened. He no longer craves sugar. When the dessert menu comes, he doesn't feel the same urge he used to feel to order something. In the afternoon, when he wants a snack, he doesn't reach for chocolate. Instead, he reaches for a banana. On the few occasions that he allows himself to indulge in sugar, it almost tastes *too* sweet. And what used to give him pleasure now no longer does—or, at least, not in the same way. He has changed.

Far be it from me to prescribe which kind of path someone needs to take toward real change. Do we wait for our hearts to be different before we start to live and act differently? Or do we start to live and act differently, even though our hearts are cold, hoping that eventually our practices and actions will warm up our hearts to see the world in different ways?

I don't know.

It's probably a bit of both. There are very godly men and

women who have written about this very conundrum, and have basically affirmed as much. Sometimes we need to wait for our hearts to change. Sometimes we need to start the walk down the road we wish to travel and allow the journey to change us with each step of the way.

In regard to prayer, I wish that I could say that my heart beams with such a love for God that the way I live my life naturally falls into godly patterns and actions. I wish I could say that, because of God's love for me, I naturally forgive my enemies, shun worry, practice gratitude, ask for the right things, pray with empathy, and never forsake the goodness of God.

But of course that's not true.

Sometimes I need my heart molded into something new, retrained into the kind of heart that God wants me to have. So sometimes I need to intentionally work certain practices into my life with the hope of seeing change follow.

Which practices should we turn to?

Here are a few that I have found to be helpful.

1. Talk to Jesus like a friend.

If the words and even the tone I use in my prayers make me sound like a different person than who I am in the rest of my conversations, I'm putting on a show. And I need to stop that. Jesus loves *me* in particular. He wants to hear from me, without any pretense or religious performance. I need to use my own words. He's not impressed with anything more than that.

2. Empty your heart.

Many times, before I can receive anything from God, I have to empty my heart first. What this means is that if I'm tired or angry or worried or even distracted, I have to first put those before God—to get them out, so to speak, so there is room for other stuff to enter. Thank God he encourages us to empty our hearts before him, in all of their rawness and honesty.

3. Listen.

Sometimes I will work through my own heart, emptying it in front of God, asking him to hear me. And then I will just sit there. I will even sometimes set a timer for ten minutes and tell God, "God, I can't make you speak to me, but I can make sure that I'm listening. These next ten minutes are yours. If you want to say anything to me, I'm listening. If not, I'm still just going to sit here and be available." Even if I leave that time of stillness feeling discouraged because I didn't hear anything from God, I can be encouraged by the fact that I'm training my heart to be still in front of him. Eventually I know that he will say something to me. But if I never give him room to speak, the chances of hearing him go way down.

4. Pray briefly, but often.

I can sometimes fall into the trap of thinking that unless I have a clearly defined time for prayer, it doesn't count for much. This couldn't be farther from the truth. Think about it like this: When one of my kids runs over from playing to give me a hug, and then almost immediately runs back to whatever he or she was doing, I don't say, "Well, that didn't count because it wasn't very long." Even in the small glances toward my direction—sometimes *especially* in the small glances toward my direction—I receive my kids' affection with gratitude and love. It's the same with God. He gets real joy whenever one of his kids looks to him, even if it's only for a quick moment.

5. If you're tired, maybe you need to go to bed.

To be sure, there are seasons in which God might move upon my heart to sacrifice sleep for the sake of gaining intimacy with him through prayer. But these are just seasons. For the most part, I know that I'm not in my best state to pray if I'm exhausted. I still feel guilt around this sometimes. I hear Jesus' words to Peter: "Could you not keep watch and pray?" But guilt is a terrible motivator for intimacy and change within a relationship. So I do my best to let that go. I try to place a value on sleep, and I pray when I'm a bit more rested.

6. Let the Bible lead.

One of my devotional practices looks like this: Before I pray, I try to read a small part of the Bible. And I do mean *small*. Maybe it's a few verses. It might be a chapter. It might even just be one verse, or even a part of a verse. The point is, I'm not reading to obtain information or to learn something. I'm reading to have my heart warmed. As soon as I come across a word or a phrase that seems like there might be some heat in it, I stop reading. I have a small journal in which I will then write down the verse or part of the verse. Then I'll pause. And pray. "God, what do you want me to hear in these words?" If something meaningful comes as an answer, I'll write that down, too. The whole process fits on a page, maybe two at the most. It's a relatively short and simple way to pray. But the point is to be present in just one thought or word that is hopefully timely and made helpful by God's Spirit.

7. Pray with others.

Several months ago a good friend came back into town. We caught up on all the happenings of our lives, laughed, and shared our hearts. Before we left each other's company, he asked if we could pray together. So there we sat, across from each other, and we prayed. He prayed that I would be a good father and husband, that I would keep working in a way that honors

God, that I would experience God's love in clear ways. And I prayed the same for him. Nothing magical happened during that time, but I did feel a sense of being known and cared for through it. And that's one of the gifts of praying with others. When God sometimes seems distant or silent, he sends one of his kids to meet with us as his representative, giving us an indication of his nearness, of his voice. Although I'm inclined to pray mostly in solitude, I have to remember that praying with others is a gift.

8. Take walks (or whatever).

In one of his writings on prayer, C. S. Lewis says that he found it helpful to pray while riding in a train.[1] For Lewis, a train car provided just enough stimulation to fend off boredom and sleepiness, but not so much stimulation that it became a distraction. I don't live near any trains, but I've found the principle to be very helpful. Sometimes I pray best in a dark room and in complete silence. But most times this kind of environment can lead to too much introspection, self-absorption, and even loneliness. If I can take a walk, or go for a hike, or even go for a drive, I find that it's easier for me to pray because I've got just the right amount of distraction to keep me focused on what I'm trying to do through prayer.

9. Remember that God knows your frame.

Psalm 103 says that God remembers who I really am—dust. I'm only human. This sounds like a cliché, but it's true: I can't be what I'm not. Only God has the creative and redemptive power to make me into something different, something new. So when I pray, I have to remember that God is the one who has the power to change me. If my desires are too small, only he can make them greater. If my heart is too broken, only he can fix it. If my will is too weak, only he can strengthen it. All that I can do is surrender.

10. Ask for help.

Of the many assurances that God gives me about prayer, these two are often the most helpful for me. First, I know that whenever I pray, God gives me his Spirit to help me. If I feel disheartened or alone or at a loss as to how I should pray, I can always look to the Spirit to help me. One of the images we have about this kind of relationship with the Spirit is that of walking with him. Or to put it another way, to *keep in step* with him. (See Galatians 5:25.) This is such a beautiful thing to think about. When I pray, the Spirit is right there, praying with me. He takes a step and then asks me to take that step with him. I have his leadership and his help.

The other help that God says I have is through Jesus. Jesus is many things to me, but in regard to prayer, it's helpful for me to remember that he is every bit my brother. He sits next to God and promises to join me in my prayers, not only praying *with* me but also praying *for* me. What a powerful image—the Son of God lifting me up in prayer to the Father, the great and true King of the universe.

So these are the things I do, or at least try to do, to grow in my relationship with God. Sometimes they work. Sometimes they even work really well. But even still, sometimes they don't. And prayer still feels like I've been dropped in a dark room without any light switches.

When all my attempts at prayer don't seem to work, though, I know (usually) that none of my efforts to understand prayer or to experience God more deeply through prayer are wasted. God tells me that, if he is anything, he is the kind of God who rewards those who seek him.

So I seek.

And I continue to seek. Because he is beautiful. Because I need him. Because I feel lost. Because he shows me enough of the way to let me know there is a way. Because beneath all of my intellect and rationale and analytical understandings of the world, I cannot shake the fact that there seems to be something transcendent behind it all. And this something seems to be somehow *personal*.

I want to know this Great Person.

And I want to be known by this Great Person.

If prayer is nothing more than this—knowing and being known by a personal God—I've learned to be okay with that. More than okay, actually. Because this is what my heart wants more than anything else.

AFTERWORD

We are, for better or for worse, different people in
different places.

—Alain de Botton[1]

Several years ago, my wife and I had the chance to go to Vail,
Colorado, for a few days in the summer. A group of pastors
were getting together and I was invited to tag along. We flew
into Denver, rented a car, and followed the highway up into the
mountains and the trees and then back down again into the
valley. I remember the golden sun and the smell of spruce and
how *clear* everything seemed to look. I felt like the man who
was born blind and then Jesus rubbed some spit and dirt into
his eyes and then he could see.

It was magnificent.

And the magnificence only continued. During one of
our free afternoons, Ashley and I packed up some water and
chocolate and granola and headed out for a hike. We drove to
a trailhead, locked up the car, and launched out into the wilderness. Over the next four hours, we treaded over trails and
rocks and fallen pine needles that whispered when we walked
on them. We crossed streams and listened to birds that we had

never heard before. We basked in the sun, and when we got too hot, we relaxed in the shade. Occasionally we saw other hikers, but for the most part it was just us, alone with each other and with nature.

This was a truly miraculous event, and not just because of the scenery. My wife has hiked exactly three times in her life. The first time was on one of our first dates. She showed up in flip-flops and a pair of cute shorts from the Gap, ready to go. Needless to say, it ended up being a short hike. The second time she hiked was when we were married and I was in graduate school. I think the only reason she agreed to it was because I said I would buy her a pair of nifty new hiking shoes. And the third was this hike in Vail.

So there I am, doing something I love, with someone I love, and I don't have a care in the world. I look up and all I see is something beautiful. I look down and I see the same thing— something beautiful. I look to my left, to my right, all around and everything I see is *beautiful*.

And it hits me.

If I lived right here, in this moment, with all of this beauty around me, my life would be different. I would be different. I would live with more kindness. More gratitude. Less anxiety. Less anger. I would be the kind of person that I so desperately want to be. I would be such a better man, a better husband, a better follower of God if I could just live right here.

Whether that's true or not, I don't know. But I do know that, every once in a while, when I'm in the mountains, or next to an ocean, or on the shore of a lake, or under an evergreen, in stillness, I get a very specific kind of a glimpse. I get a glimpse into how life might be if I could just live somewhere else than where I usually am. When I'm in these kinds of places, I feel more at peace. I feel less confusion. I feel more compassion for the world, and less desire to control it. I feel hopeful. My heart feels alive.

But then I leave these other places and the truth about my heart comes rushing back. And the truth is my heart is a wreck. It wants what it shouldn't want and doesn't want what it should. It tricks me. It is overly sensitive at times, woefully insensitive at others. It is exceptionally good at worshipping the wrong things and tragically bad at worshipping the right things. It is lazy. And angry. And selfish. And cold.

But when I'm in one of these peaceful places of relief, none of this matters. There I am, wrecked heart and all, and I'm *okay*. I become a different person in these different places, even if it's only for a moment. My soul's attention moves away from its own deficiencies and instead turns toward the beauty that's around it. I forget about my guilt. And all I can see is mercy.

This is my greatest hope in prayer.

Beyond all my feelings of struggle and weakness, I hope that prayer becomes the kind of place in my life where I can remember that all is grace, God is mercy, and I am loved.

Nothing more, and nothing less, will do for my needy heart.

I am praying the same for you.

ACKNOWLEDGMENTS

To my parents: Dad, you instilled in me a love for written words from a very young age. Mom, one of my earliest memories is seeing you in the morning light with a Bible in your lap, praying. These written words on prayer are proud tributes to you both.

To the rest of my family: Thank you for love and patience with me as I grew up, and as I continue to grow today.

To my friends: Each of you has, in your own way, carried me. I am grateful.

To the staff, elders, and congregation at Grace: It is a great joy and privilege to follow Jesus in your midst. Thank you for your love, and for your trust.

To Alex, Keren, and Grace: Your belief in this project is a gift. Thank you for your support and kindness.

To the A's: Daddy loves all of you more than these small words can contain. Your smiles teach me more about prayer than any book or sermon ever could.

To Ashley: Without you, I would be a lonely shadow, a much poorer version of who I am today. Your light, your love, your yes to me these many years ago. I love you.

NOTES

INTRODUCTION MAKING ROOM

1. Georges Bernanos, *The Diary of a Country Priest* (Cambridge, Mass.: Da Capo Press, 1965), 103.

CHAPTER 1 FRIENDSHIP

1. Brennan Manning, *The Ragamuffin Gospel* (Colorado Springs: Multnomah Books, 2005), 25.
2. Walt Whitman, "Song of Myself," https://www.poetryfoundation.org/poems/45477/song-of-myself-1892-version.
3. Peter Kreeft, *Prayer for Beginners* (San Francisco: Ignatius, 2000), 25,

CHAPTER 2 REACHING

1. C. S. Lewis, *Mere Christianity* (San Francisco: HarperSanFrancisco, 2001), Chapter 1.
2. Ibid., 8.

CHAPTER 3 DISTRACTIONS

1. At the time of writing, we had three children. Since the time of writing, we added a fourth.

CHAPTER 4 GUILT

1. Augustine, *Confessions*, Book 1.

CHAPTER 5 GRATITUDE

1. Jim Manney, *A Simple Life-Changing Prayer* (Chicago: Loyola Press, 2011), 34.

CHAPTER 6 DISAPPOINTMENT

1. The show I'm talking about is from Netflix's *Chef's Table*, Season 3, Episode 6: "Virgilio Martinez."
2. This is an often-cited story and I have read it in various places. For the sake of ease, it appears here: https://www.desiringgod.org/articles/dwight-l-moody-turns-172.
3. Anselm makes these arguments in his famous work, *The Proslogion*.
4. C. S. Lewis, *Mere Christianity* (San Francisco: HarperSanFrancisco, 2001), 136–37.
5. ———, *The Screwtape Letters* (New York: Touchstone, 1996), 42.

CHAPTER 7 OTHERS

1. The documentary I'm talking about is from Netflix's *Abstract*, Season 1, Episode 8: "Ilse Crawford: Interior Design."
2. M. Scott Peck, *The Road Less Traveled* (New York: Touchstone, 2003), 15.
3. Donald Miller, *Scary Close* (Nashville: Thomas Nelson, 2015), 113.
4. Peter Kreeft, *Making Sense Out of Suffering* (Cincinnati: Servant Books, 1986), 10.

CHAPTER 9 SILENCE

1. Eugene H. Peterson, *Answering God: The Psalms as Tools for Prayer* (New York: HarperOne, 1989).

CHAPTER 10 AWARENESS

1. Brother Lawrence and Frank Laubach, *Practicing His Presence* (Sargent, Ga.: The Seedsowers, 1973), 71.
2. Ibid., 99–100.
3. Ibid., 2–3.
4. Ibid., 5.
5. David Foster Wallace, *This Is Water: Some Thoughts, Delivered on a Significant Occasion, about Living a Compassionate Life* (New York: Little, Brown and Company, 2009), 3–8.

CHAPTER 11 REPENTANCE

1. I am attempting to summarize one of the key arguments and foundations of Plato here. The best place to read them for yourself is *The Republic*.

2. C. S. Lewis, *Mere Christianity* (San Francisco: HarperSanFrancisco, 2001), 136–37.

CHAPTER 12 FORGIVENESS

1. Anne Lamott, *Traveling Mercies: Some Thoughts on Faith* (New York: Anchor, 2000), 120.

CHAPTER 13 PAIN

1. Alain de Botton, *The Architecture of Happiness* (New York: Vintage International, 2008), 22–25.

CHAPTER 15 SIMPLE

1. W. H. Lewis, ed., *Letters of C. S. Lewis* (New York: Harvest Books, 1966), 165.

AFTERWORD

1. Alain de Botton, *The Architecture of Happiness* (New York: Vintage International, 2008), 13.

ABOUT THE AUTHOR

Adam Dressler is the Lead Pastor of Grace Community Church in Clarksville, Tennessee.

Adam earned his bachelor's degree in theology from Oral Roberts University. Following ORU, he graduated from Harvard Divinity School with an MTS in Christianity and culture.

He and his wife, Ashley, live in Clarksville, where they are raising their four young children.